Paris For Kids

Paris For Kids

Karen Uhlmann

Photography by Alexander Uhlmann

Copyright © 2005 by Karen Uhlmann.

Library of Congress Number: 2002095600
ISBN: Hardcover 1-4010-8050-2
Softcover 1-4010-8049-9

All rights reserved. No part of this book may be reproduced or transmitted in any form or by any means, electronic or mechanical, including photocopying, recording, or by any information storage and retrieval system, without permission in writing from the copyright owner.

This book was printed in the United States of America.

To order additional copies of this book, contact:
Xlibris Corporation
1-888-795-4274
www.Xlibris.com
Orders@Xlibris.com

Dedication

To My Traveling Companions: Tom, Alexander,
Evan and Gregory

Traveling with children is never easy. For a few years, I felt I could barely take mine to the grocery store. But because I lived in and travel frequently to Paris, my three boys began to beg. They were thirteen, ten, and almost seven years old. I talked it up, using it as a frequent threat, "Children who behave like you do certainly can't go to Paris." I became more and more convinced I was making a terrible mistake. But they really wanted to go. I took a deep breath and we went. And they loved it. It was a completely different type of trip than one I would have taken. And it was wonderful to see Paris through their eyes.

I think that people are more afraid of taking children to Paris than other cities. Parisians are stereotyped as unfriendly (not true), and Paris is perceived as an "adult city". There are a lot of children living in and around Paris and tons of wonderful, kid-centered activities. There are also the museums and monuments, which my kids liked in small doses. The key is combining museum trips with park like activities.

Since it seems that many Parisians take their dogs out to dinner and leave their children at home, where we stayed and ate was a big consideration. We needed kid-friendly hotels, restaurants, and activities. Feeling welcome makes all the difference in the world. And for the most part, we did. The only person who ever said anything nasty to us was American.

We stayed in a hotel that was terrific with the kids, and all the hotels in this book liked having children as guests. The biggest challenge was eating out. If your children are willing to sit for a three-course dinner, and you are willing to pay for them as adults, by all means go to nice bistros. French children (especially small ones) do not go out a lot, except for special occasions. Children are expected to be quiet and well behaved (mini-adults). Even my kids rose to the standards, although we occasionally brought GameBoy to the table. Ethnic restaurants and smaller casual places are also excellent choices, especially for the squirmy and squeamish. Domino's and Pizza Hut both deliver in Paris. There was one night I was very grateful for this. Otherwise, I think it's nice for kids to discover what they like (or don't like) about French food.

Beyond the basics, kid travel has different considerations. How do you get around with a stroller? Do juice boxes exist in Paris? What are the French words for disposable diapers (*couches à jeter*)? What if you need a pediatrician? The right information can make all the difference between a wonderful, calm trip and a stressful trip. This book is geared toward people somewhat like me. I wouldn't stay at the Bristol, but I want hotel rooms to be pretty and comfortable, and I like to go to nice bistros for dinner. I am not the type to throw my family into a van and wing it through Europe, sharing beds, and staying in youth hostels. At the same time, I prefer not to spend a fortune on hotels. Decide what is most important to you.

It helped my children enormously to know what to expect. Because we live in a city, we were able to go to French bistros several times with them before the trip. We talked about how French children tend to be quieter. Screaming across the métro at your brother is not cool. Neither is running hell-bent down a street.

It fascinated them that you can't just plop down in an empty, outdoor café table without ordering something – and that there were no other children in the restaurants. It also helped to explain that when you go out to dinner, you are expected to order "normally," in other words, like an adult. You can't just have bread and cheese or potatoes for dinner most places, although every restaurant was willing to accommodate my teenage vegetarian. One of the high points of their trip was when they saw two French boys spitting off a balcony down to the street. No one's perfect.

Contents

Helpful Hints Before You Start 11

Arrival in Paris 14

Things I Wish People Had Told Me 16

Kid Picks 23

Treasure Hunt 27

Survival Guide: Food Facts 30

The Lay of the Land 38

Hotels 45

Restaurants 65

France 101 83

Just For Kids: Amusement Parks 89

Parks and Playgrounds 95

Monuments 102

Museums 111

Zoos 127

Oddball Activities 130

Boat Trips 133

Fun Fairs 135

Toy Stores 136

Clothing Stores 140

Just in Case You Need It: Health 145

Helpful Hints Before You Start

Talk with your kids about the trip and ask what they want to see. Chances are, the Eiffel Tower and the *Mona Lisa* will be at the top of their lists. Read them the French history section from this book. The French Revolution (blood and guts) is tremendously appealing. The sights are way more interesting if children know what actually happened at them.

✧ Let each child plan a day of things they want to do and see. Give her or him a map, and have them highlight how to get to these places. It may not be possible to do everything in one day, but looking at a map helps a kid see the feasibility of choices.

✧ Try to choose an airline with in-seat TVs (most Boeing 777s). Many offer these in coach, and it really helps the whole family have a peaceful plane ride.

✧ Buy each child a journal and a glue stick, so he or she can keep a scrapbook of the trip. It's fun to glue in museum stubs, restaurant cards, and used métro tickets. We've provided a checklist – a Parisian treasure hunt, but you can also create your own.

✧ Read to them, or have them read a few books that take place in Paris. Older kids might enjoy *The Hunchback of Notre Dame*. Younger ones will like the *Madeline* series and *Eloise in Paris*.

- Buy disposable cameras or film for your children here. It's easier and less expensive.

- Set some limits in advance. For instance, we will go to Disneyland, but we are also going to three museums of our choice. At the museums, you may pick out your five favorite paintings and we will buy postcards of them on our way out.

- If possible, introduce your children to some French foods ahead of time. It will let them know what to expect and give them something tangible to be excited about. French meals, even in bistros, are three courses. The first course is called an *entrée*, the second a *plat*, dessert, and then coffee. Cheese is served either before, or instead of, dessert.

- Familiarize yourself with a map of the area in which you are staying. If you have young children who will be exhausted at the end of the day, you may want to choose nearby restaurants. It's always better to know that you have a reservation, so fax your choices and dates to your hotel before your trip.

- Bring an empty rolled-up, duffel bag to put all your laundry in, as it won't be convenient to do it in Paris. This way, it's all in one place, and the suitcases have room for purchases.

- Make two photocopies of everyone's passport. Leave one set at home in an easy-to-find place, and take one set of copies with you. Put these in a separate place from where you have the passports. This will make your passports easier to replace, should anything happen to them.

- Check with your bank, but many ATMs in Paris are accessible with Cirrus PLUS or Visa cash cards. The exchange rate is much better than what you get if you change dollars or cash travelers checks. You will pay a fee to use your card (and interest, if you use a charge account for cash), but it will be nominal, and you can get the exact fee amount from your bank in advance. This is the easiest way to get cash as you need it.

✧ Bring all medications with you, so that you don't get frantic and waste time and energy hunting them down if someone gets a cough, cold, or fever. I also pack some Band-Aids and Neosporin.

✧ Pack your GameBoys for those tired and tense moments.

✧ Bring your Swiss Army knife (although not on the plane). It is very handy for picnics and opening bottles of wine.

✧ This may sound silly, but buy a lot of pre-packaged wipes and carry some in your purse. Between the cotton candy, ice cream, and dirt in the parks, you'll need them, especially in the summer. Dirt sticks to cotton candy residue.

✧ Now that I've said pack everything, don't panic if you forget a few items. This is Paris; baby shampoo, Band-Aids, and diapers are readily available.

Arrival in Paris

I used to say that the simplest thing to do was hire a van service. This is because taxis legally only have to take three passengers (although children under ten count as half). However, both shuttle services have proved themselves unreliable. I now think it's better to get in the taxi line and wait for a taxi van. If you use a van, you won't have the expense of two taxis (which is at least 35 € – and probably more – from Charles De Gaulle). If you want to take your chances, I'm providing van information. But I absolutely wouldn't advise taking one back to the airport for your return flight. You could risk missing your plane. Also, leave for Charles De Gaulle three hours before your flight as it takes a long time to check in and pass through all the security.

Parishuttle

Internet site: www.parishuttle.com
Tel: 011-33-1-53-39-18-18 (The first numbers 011 33 are the country code. Drop these and add a 0 before the 1 if you're in Paris.)
Fax: 011-33-1-53-39-13-13

If you are alone, this shuttle service will cost 25 €. However, for two to five people, the per-person cost is 18 € and with five to eight people, the cost drops to 15 € per person. Children three to ten are 10 € and children under three are free. You can make and have your reservations confirmed by E-mail. At the airport, you dial a toll-free number for pickup, and they will tell you where to meet the van. This is not private, so you will be riding with and dropping off other passengers.

Airport Shuttle

Internet site: www.paris-anglo.com/airport_shuttles.php

A single person is 22 €, two or more people are 14.50 € each, and children under three are free. Reserve ahead and dial a toll-free number at the airport. This is also not private, and you may be riding with and dropping off other passengers.

Taxi

There are plenty of taxis at both airports. Charles De Gaulle Airport is about sixteen miles northeast of the city. The fare will be at least 35 € (and probably more), and higher after 8 p.m. Orly is about nine miles south of Paris, and the charges will probably be about 22-25.15 €. There is a charge for each suitcase that needs to go into the trunk (currently .90 €).

Things I Wish People Had Told Me

- ✧ The Office de Tourisme de Paris
  127 av. des Champs-Elysées
  75008 Paris
  Tel: 08-92-68-31-12
  Métro: Charles-de-Gaulle-Etoille
  Hours: 9 a.m. to 8 p.m. daily (except May 1)
  This is an extremely helpful place. The multilingual staff can answer your questions, and the office is one-stop shopping for phone cards, museum cards, travel passes, and various other museum and theater tickets. The office has a hotel reservation service, and a small bank for changing money as well as brochures on attractions and events.

- ✧ You need a phone card to use a payphone. It's 7.50 € for fifty units and 15.40 € for a 120-unit card. Each unit is good for a local call of six to eighteen minutes depending on the rate. The cards are for sale at *tabacs* (tobacco shops), newspaper shops and post offices, some tourist offices, and France Telecom stores. The directions for the phone will be written in French on a small screen. You can do it. *Décrochez* means pick up the receiver, *insertez votre carte* means insert your card (with the arrow up and the way the arrow is pointing), *numérotez* means dial, and *raccrochez* means hang up. The line clicks until it rings.

- Buy a *Paris Par Arrondissement* immediately at a newsstand or bookstore. This is a small map book that enables you to look up locations by street and arrondissement. It has a métro map in the back. Paris has a lot of small, winding streets. Even Parisians carry them.

- Taxis wait at taxi stands (*stations de taxi*). You may hail them on the street if they have all three roof lights on and they are at least fifty meters from a stand, but this can be difficult. Check with your hotel for the closest stand. If you call a taxi, the taxi charges from the moment it leaves to come pick you up. So there can be a hefty amount on the meter before you even get in. If you do find one on the street or at a stand, there is a beginning meter charge that is currently 2.30 €.

- Now that I've told you about taxis, face the fact that you can't count on getting one. This is especially true during rush hour which may be when you're trying to leave for dinner. It's generally easy to call a taxi from the restaurant to return to your hotel. Also, remember, taxis legally only have to take three. Children under ten count as half. Occasionally, drivers will ask you where you're going then zip off when you answer. Don't take it personally. It just means that they're done for the day (or night), and you're not on their way home.

- The métro is the fastest, easiest, and cheapest way to get around. A *carnet* (ten tickets) is 9.30 €. Children's carnets are 4.65 € (for kids under eleven). Three-year-olds and under ride free. You may also buy a two-, three-, or five-day pass. This is far simpler than constantly stopping to buy métro tickets. You can choose either three or five zones. If you are planning to take the métro to Disneyland make sure you buy a five-zone. If not, it's cheaper to buy a three-zone, and pay a supplement for Disneyland and Versailles. These passes are good for all types of Paris transportation, including the bus, tram, Montmartre funicular, and on the RER. Please note that they have to be used over consecutive days.

There is a métro map on the wall of the station, and free for asking at the ticket booths. Save yourself time and stress by plotting your trip out before you go rather than with your children screaming at you in the métro station.

Look at a métro map. You need to know the number of the line you are taking and its last stop. Figure this out before you get on, or you'll be sorry – and lost. If you were going from Concorde to Bastille, you would be taking line one in the direction of Château Vincennes. Each direction is clearly marked with the stops, listed underneath. You often have to change lines to get where you need to go, which is no big deal if you know the connecting line number and its last stop (which is the direction). Trains come every few minutes. If you are using regular métro tickets, hold on to them until you reach your destination. Train officials may randomly inspect tickets, and if you don't have one, you can be fined, and hauled in if you don't have the cash with you to pay the fine.

Zone 1 to 3 includes Paris and the nearby suburbs (La Défense, Le Bourget and Saint-Denis Basilique). There is a five-zone pass that will get you to Disneyland and the airport, but it's more economical to buy the three-zone and pay for the long trips.

Pass for one day and three zones: 8.50 €
Pass for two days and three zones: 13.80 €
Pass for three days and three zones: 18.40 €
Children four to eleven are half price.

- ✧ If you're really enterprising, bring small headshots about the size of a passport photo. Then buy each family member a weekly (Monday to Monday) Carte Orange. It's 13.20 € and allows unlimited métro use within Paris. Children are the same price as adults. The Carte Orange for each week is sold through Wednesday.

- ✧ When you take to the RER or SCNF trains (to Disneyland and Versailles), you need to look for the name of the train going to your destination on the monitor. If you get on a train that just looks like it has your stop written on the front, it may be the wrong one. While the five-zone passes allow you to ride in the first-class RER and SCNF compartments, the supplemental ticket you buy to travel with your three-zone pass does not. Sit in second class. Train officials frequently come through and check tickets, and you can be fined.

✧ Have your children carry a piece of the hotel notepaper with the phone number and address on it, just in case they should ever get lost.

✧ Always put change in an outside pocket. The portable, self-cleaning toilets along the streets are .50 €. These toilets were a big item. They have doors that slide open when money is inserted, and showers that clean the bathrooms with a big whoosh afterwards. This whoosh is the entire compartment being raised to the ceiling and cleaned. This is why you must accompany children under ten. The electronic sensor can miss them, and they'll be raised and sanitized along with the toilet. I learned this from a toilet repairman when I was about to let my seven-year-old go in alone.

✧ Whatever you have forgotten is at the Monoprix. These are huge cheap stores that are everywhere. They carry baby bottles, diapers, deodorant, toothpaste, brushes, and clothes. Most also have huge supermarkets inside. My favorite socks are from here; they have fantastic underwear and a good line of cheap makeup called Bourjois. Moms need stuff too.

✧ If your rental car breaks down (*une panne*) on the highway, you need to call the French police in order to get towed. Dial 17 from the nearest emergency telephone box. The police need to phone a garage and authorize towing. You have to call; the agency can't. Scream at them later.

✧ Breakfast in most hotels is very expensive. And, it's even more so if your kids want something other than croissants and French bread. Orange juice is often an extra charge, even if the breakfast is included in the room rate. However, orange juice can be picked up cheaply at any grocery store. One alternative is to breakfast in a café. However, if this is going to be an enormous hassle, you can book a hotel where breakfast is included, or just bite the bullet and pay the high prices.

✧ Long distance carrier codes:

MCI: 08-00-99-00-19
Sprint: 08-00-99-00-87
AT&T: 08-00-99-00-11

These can all be directly accessed from pay phones without a phone card.

✧ Paris can pour, but it also frequently drips. If you go in the spring, the weather will probably be cold and damp at least part of the time. It can be sunny when you leave your hotel and start drizzling after you've walked just a few blocks. If your visit is in the winter or spring, bring waterproof shoes or boots, coats, and umbrellas, or you'll be wet all day.

✧ *Pariscope* is a weekly guide to everything in Paris that can be purchased at any newsstand. It comes out every Wednesday. There is always a section devoted to kids, although it is in French. There is also a small section in English called "Time Out." Although it's not necessarily about kids, it gives explanations that will help you understand the French listing.

✧ The French are more formal than we are, so you need to follow protocol if you don't want to be rude. It's simple. When you enter a store or restaurant say, "*Bonjour, Madame*" or "*Bonjour, Monsieur.*" When you leave, it's "*Au revoir, Madame*" (or *Monsieur*). If you have bought something, be sure and say, "*Merci.*" The same greeting is appropriate for the staff at hotels. It's nice if you at least try to speak French. A little politeness goes a long way.

✧ There is much less sense of personal space in Paris than in the U.S. People walk closely, crowd together on the métro, and sit at tightly spaced tables. It may seem that people are on top of you, but chalk it up to a cultural difference and tight space.

✧ If you have a stroller-aged child, invest in a light, easy-to-fold umbrella stroller. This way you will be able to both walk and get on and off the métro. You need the lightest stroller you can find, as you will be carrying it up and down endless stairs in métro stations. Paris involves more walking than most children are used to doing, so if you're in doubt pack it.

✧ Poop alert. Dogs rule here, and their owners do not clean up after them. It's everywhere – so watch it.

✧ In good weather, plan picnics. Going to an outdoor market or a French supermarket is an adventure. There's nothing like checking out the cookies and chips in a different language. Picnics are inexpensive, less stressful, and everyone can choose what they want. If you're trying to save money, drinks and waters will be a lot cheaper in the supermarkets than at the street stands.

- ✧ If you can work in a little shopping, Au Printemps (64 bd. Hausseman, 75009, métro: Havre Caumartin) has an enormous perfume and makeup counter, as well as clothes and accessories for everyone. It's speedy one-stop shopping, and if you spend more than 175 €, you can fill out the VAT tax forms for a refund in a comfortable chair. On Thursdays, the store is open up to 10:00 p.m. Bon Marché, my favorite department store (24 rue des Sèvres, 75006, Metro: Sévres-Babylone), is open until 9 p.m. on Thursday. You could feed everyone early, let your husband stay home, and nab a few hours for yourself.

- ✧ Do what's fun. Wander down the banks of the Seine and look at houseboats. Get an ice cream cone. Take a pony ride. Save the sightseeing marathon for an adult trip. Slow down and let your kids absorb the culture and learn to love new places.

Kid Picks

✧ The Bateaux-Mouches – an hour boat ride around the Seine. It's a great overview, plus it's a boat, and how fun is that. In the winter, it's warm inside, but the river walls in some places will block your view. Explanations are given in many languages, and your kids can choose to listen or not.

✧ The Eiffel Tower. Visit in the afternoon when the line is not as long. There is a choice of three different levels by stairs or elevator. Go to the top. The view on a clear day is at least fifty miles. If your kids are up late, the view at night is spectacular.

✧ Jardin d'Acclimatation. This wonderful, low-key amusement park in the Bois de Boulogne has everything from rides, to a children's museum, to miniature golf. There is even a small zoo. It's open daily year-round and is definitely a big hit.

✧ The Ferris wheel at the Place Concorde. This is set up for Christmas and it is free, although you have to stand in a long line. It's also operating during the summer, as part of La Fête des Tuileries from mid-June through late August. The view from here at night is also spectacular. During December, you can see the Christmas lights down the Champs-Elysées and all over the city.

✧ The merry-go-rounds *(manèges)*. Paris is carousel crazy. Free merry-go-rounds are set up in St. Sulpice, Concorde, and Place de Hôtel de La Ville for Christmas and for various festivals during the summer. There is a permanent merry-go-round at the foot of the Eiffel Tower, a double-decker carousel at the base of the steps to Sacré Coeur, and a regular merry-go-round in the Place de Batignolles (17th Arrondissement). Merry-go-rounds are in nearly every park. Here are a few: an antique carousel in the Butte de Chaumont (19th Arrondissement), Parc Monceau, Champ de Mars, Tuileries and Luxembourg Gardens.

- ✧ Chocolate *macarons* from Laudurée. Voted the best in Paris by my family. These are not like our coconut macaroons. The French chocolate cookies are a sandwich of almond and chocolate cookies with a chocolate filling. There are many other flavors. Coffee *(café)* is our runner-up. This is also a great place to eat breakfast if you are staying in a hotel where breakfast is not included. It is like an old-fashioned tearoom, and I think that Lauderée's croissants are the best in Paris. Addresses: 16 rue Royale, 8th Arrondissement, 75 av. Champs Elysées, 8th Arrondissement, 21 rue Bonaparte, 6th arrondissement, and in the department store Le Printemps, 64, bd. Haussmann, 9th Arrondisement.

- ✧ Ice cream at Berthillon. Although you can have Berthillon ice cream at many cafés, it's more fun to go there. It is located at 31 rue St.-Louis-en-l'Ile. This is a perfect time to soak up this tiny island's unique charm. There are plain, as well as exotic, flavors to choose from. Ile St.-Louis is right behind Nôtre Dame, so this is a perfect bribe to follow a cathedral visit. This is a great Sunday destination, as many of the shops on the island are open – and stores are closed in most of Paris. Berthillon is closed Monday and Tuesday, and, unbelievably, the last half of July and all of August. Berthillon's hours are 10 a.m. to 8 p.m.

- ✧ Hot chocolate in the tearoom at Jean-Paul Hévin, 231 rue St-Honoré, 75001. It's like drinking liquid, bittersweet chocolate. Afterwards, you can buy some to take home in the gorgeous chocolate shop downstairs. Don't miss their *macarons,* especially the *"ancien."* They have two other locations – 3 rue Vavin, 75006 and 16 av. de la Motte-Picquet, 75007.

- ✧ The Buci market. A large, colorful outdoor market on rue Buci and rue de Seine. Fruits and vegetables are piled high on tables that line both streets. Stop and buy some fruit from a vendor. Check out the cheese and the line-up of flowers in buckets. It's the perfect place to pick up sandwiches, quiches, or minipizzas for lunch. They even sell drinks (as does the supermarket on the corner). Carton, an excellent *pâtisserie*, is also located on rue de Buci. It is guaranteed to make everyone happy. (Métro: Saint-Germain-des-Prés)

- ✧ The bird market on the Ile de la Cité. The flower market is open daily, but on Sundays (9 a.m. to 7 p.m.) exotic flowers are replaced by birds, rabbits, ferrets, and even an occasional beaver. Warning: I've seen rabbits bite.

- ✧ The Musée D'Orsay. Besides the fabulous Impressionist and post-Impressionist collection, it is one of the most beautiful buildings in the world. Pick what you want to see – and it's totally manageable.

- ✧ All the Paris playgrounds.

Treasure Hunt

How cool would it be to have a scrapbook of your trip to show your friends and keep forever? Bring a notebook or journal, glue stick, your camera or a disposable one (or two). Polaroid also makes a small camera that takes tiny pictures with self-sticking backs. These are wonderful, because the pictures can be inserted daily. Search for these things and you'll have a great memory book.

Two used Paris métro tickets

One Eiffel Tower entrance stub

Bateau-Mouche ticket

Three postcards of your favorite paintings

Three postcards of your favorite sites

Card from the best pâtisserie with the name of your pastry written on it

Snapshots of your family and important places (to you) in Paris

A picture of a dog at a restaurant

A museum ticket – it can be your parents' ticket as children get in free to many museums

Card from your two favorite restaurants and what you had to eat written underneath

A métro map (ask at your hotel or métro station)

A snapshot of your favorite playground

A piece of your hotel note paper

Anything else you can think of

Survival Guide: Food Facts

Breakfast (*Petit Déjeuner*):

Breakfast in France is almost always the same anywhere, be it at your hotel or café.

Croissant – a buttery, crescent-shaped roll
Brioche – a buttery, yeasty egg roll which looks like a little hat
Petit pain – French bread roll
Pain au chocolat – croissant with chocolate inside
Pain au raisins – little, sweet pastry with raisins
Confiture – jam
Beurre – butter
Chocolat – hot chocolate
Café au lait – coffee with warm milk
Café crème – the same thing
Café noir – black coffee
Thé – tea
Jus d'orange – orange juice

To Market to Market

Fruits (des fruits):

Abricot – apricot
Banane – banana
Cerise – cherry
Clémentine – small seedless orange
Figue – fig
Fraise – strawberry
Framboise – raspberry
Orange – orange
Mirabelle – yellow plum
Myrtille – blueberry
Pamplemousse – grapefruit
Pêche – peach
Poire – pear
Pomme – apple
Prune – plum
Raisin – grape

Vegetables (legumes):

This is good to know for take-out salads

Artichaut – artichoke
Asperge – asparagus
Aubergine – eggplant
Carotte – carrot
Céleri – celery (try celery *rémoulade*, a delicious celery root and mayonnaise salad from a *traiteur* – a take-out gourmet)
Champignon – mushroom
Courgette – zucchini
Haricot vert – green bean
Pommes de terre – potato

Gratin dauphinoise – baked cheese and potato casserole often available at *traiteurs* (take-out gourmet)

Sandwiches:

Croque-monsieur – toasted ham and cheese sandwich
Croque-madame – same as above with an egg
Fromage – cheese
Jambon – ham
Oeuf – egg
Du thon – tuna
Poulet – chicken
Saucisson – salami
Saumon fumé – smoked salmon

Quiche:

Epinards – spinach
Poireau – leek
Saumon – salmon
Lorraine – cheese and bacon
Fromage – cheese

Bread (pain):

Baguette – what we think of as French bread
Pain de campagne – country bread
Pain complet – whole-wheat
Pain de mie – sandwich bread
Petit pain – roll
Pain de seigle – rye bread

Chocolate:

Chocolat – chocolate
Chocolat au lait – milk chocolate

Chocolate noir – bittersweet chocolate
Chocolate amer – bittersweet chocolate with extra sugar

Drinks (boissons):

Badoit – fizzy mineral water
Coca – Coke
Citron Pressé – lemon juice that you add water and sugar to, before you drink it to make lemonade
Eau – water
Evian – flat mineral water
Fanta – orange soda
Jus d'orange – orange juice
Lait – milk
Orange Pressé – orange juice that you add water and sugar to for a sweet drink
Orangina – fizzy orange drink
Perrier – fizzy mineral water
Vichy – flat mineral water
Vin – wine
Rouge – red
Blanc – white

Dinner (dîner):

These are just the basics. There are hundreds of preparations, all with different names, so don't be afraid to ask your waiter if he or she can explain a dish.

A typical French dinner is an *entrée* (first course), *plat* (main course), and dessert. Sometimes cheese is served instead of or before the dessert course. Coffee is served after dessert and is always espresso. Most restaurants have decaf.

Meat (les viandes):

Bifteck – beef steak

Côte d'agneau – lamb chop
Côte de bœuf – usually a rib steak
Côte de porc – pork chop
Côte de veau – veal chop
Cassoulet – a bean, duck, and lamb casserole
Châteaubriand – a thick steak
Daube – stew (often beef)
Entrecôte – beef rib steak
Lapin – bunny
Foie – liver
Foie gras – duck liver
Gigot – leg of lamb
Moelle – beef marrow
Onglet – a slightly better cut of beef than a flank steak
Pâté – a mixture of spiced meats usually served before dinner
Steak au poivre – pepper steak
Tournedos – the center portion of a filet of beef

Poultry (volaille):

Cuisee means leg and *aile* means wing
Canard – duck
Caille – quail
Faisan – pheasant
Poulet – chicken
Dindon – turkey
Pintade – guinea fowl
Poussin – baby chicken

Potatoes (pommes de terre):

Frites – fries
Dauphinoise – sliced potatoes, milk and cheese
Duchesse – mashed potatoes
Lyonnaise – sautéed potatoes with onions

Vapeur – steamed
A l'anglaise – boiled

Lettuce (laitue):

Frisé – curly lettuce
Endive – chicory
Mâche – lamb's lettuce
Salade verte – green salad

Fish (poisson):

Barbue – a mild Mediterranean fish
Belon – a type of flat-shelled oyster
Brandade de morue – a puree of salt cod, garlic, milk, and potatoes (it looks like mashed potatoes)
Cabillaud – cod
Coquillages – shellfish
Coquilles Saint-Jacques – scallops
Crabe – crab
Crevette – shrimp
Daurade – sea bream
Fruits de mer – seafood
Homard – lobster
Huître – oyster
Langoustine – prawn
Lieu – pollack
Lotte – monkfish
Loup – common Mediterranean fish that is a bit like sea bass
Moules – mussels
Perche – perch
Rouget – red mullet
Saint-Pierre – mild white fish
Sandre – a freshwater fish that is similar to *perche*
Saumon – salmon (fumé – smoked)

Tourteau – crab (not to be confused with *tortue* which is turtle)
Truite – trout
Turbot – turbot

Desserts (déserts):

Biscuit – cookie
Charlotte aux Pommes – a warm, molded apple cake
Charlotte au chocolat – a molded chocolate cream cake surrounded by a layer of ladyfingers
Clafoutis – this is sweetened batter poured over fruit placed in a baking dish. It looks like a tart with the fruit baked in and is usually served warm.
Crème brûlée – a custard in a porcelain dish topped with caramelized sugar
Crème caramel – caramel custard
Crêpe – thin pancake usually filled with sugar, chocolate or fruit for dessert
Gâteau – cake (look for the word *chocolat* with it)
Gaufre – a waffle usually topped with whipped cream (chantilly) or ice cream
Glace – ice cream
Ile flottante (floating island) or *oeufs a la neige* – soft meringues sitting in a vanilla – custard sauce – kids often don't like the consistency

Macarons – amazing cookies that are crisp on the outside and soft on the inside often sandwiched together with a filling

Madeleine – a shell-shaped sponge cake cookie

Marjolaine – a layered chocolate nut cake

Marquise au chocolate – a chocolate mousse cake

Mont Blanc – ice cream or a meringue with candied, chestnut puree and whipped cream

Mousse – a rich pudding which is often chocolate

Pithiviers – puff pastry filled with an almond cream

Poires Belle Hélène – poached pears with vanilla ice cream and chocolate sauce

Pot-de-crème – a very rich custard in a cup

Profiteroles – puff pastries filled with whipped cream or ice cream and topped with chocolate sauce

Reine de Saba – a chocolate cake with a creamy center. It's usually frosted with chocolate butter cream and decorated with almonds

Religieuse – two puff pastries, one on top of the other, filled with chocolate or coffee cream and frosted with chocolate or coffee

Riz au lait – rice pudding

Sablés – rich, buttery sugar cookies

Tarte – open-faced pie filled with pastry cream (like vanilla pudding but better) and topped with fruit

Tarte aux fruits – mixed fruit

Tarte aux pommes – apple

Tarte aux fraises – strawberry

Tarte aux abricots – apricot tart

Tarte au citons – lemon tart

Tarte aux poires – pear tart

Tarte au fromage frais – sweet cream cheese tart which tastes like cheesecake

Tarte Tatin – a caramelized upside-down apple tart

The Lay of the Land

***Arrondissements*:** Paris is divided into twenty arrondissements or sections. The first arrondissement is the center of the city, with the others laid out clockwise around it. They are generally referred to just by their number (14), or with an *e* at the end (14e). The last two digits of a Paris address give the arrondissement. For instance, 75011 would be in the 11th Arrondissement. To understand Paris, it helps to comprehend the flavor of each arrondissement. This will also help you pick the neighborhood you would like to stay in.

First Arrondissement

Here's where you'll find Chanel, Courréges, Annick Goutal, as well as the amazing collection of souvenir shops along rue de Rivoli (it's one after the other). The first and the eighth arrondissements have the big-name shopping streets. The Louvre is also in the first, as well as part of the Tuileries and the Palais Royal.

Second Arrondissement

The Place Vendôme crosses over to the second arrondissement, which is called La Bourse. The bulk of the arrondissement is the garment center, which will probably not interest you. There are, however, some lovely hotels in the second, near the area bordering the first arrondissement.

Third Arrondissement

This area is called the Marais, and it has become very chic over the past couple of years. The Picasso Museum is here, and the Place des Vosges (one of the oldest and most beautiful squares in Paris) is on the border of the third and fourth arrondissement.

In both the third and fourth arrondisements, which make up the Marais, there are lots of little boutiques and bistros. Shops are often open here on Sundays when everything else is closed.

Fourth Arrondissement

This area has experienced a major renaissance over the past couple of years. It is full of ultra-hip boutiques. The Jewish Quarter, which is an old Jewish neighborhood with shops and restaurants, is also here. The fourth is interesting because it includes Paris's two islands – Ile de la Cité (Nôtre Dame) and Ile St.-Louis. The Ile de la Cité is where Paris was originally settled.

Fifth Arrondissement

The Latin Quarter. It's full of students, bookstores, and ethnic restaurants. Kids like the restaurants and the liveliness.

Sixth Arrondissement

My personal favorite. Here you'll find the Buci Market and the Luxembourg Gardens. It's full of chic boutiques and cafés like Café Flore and Deux Magots. It is also an area with a concentration of antique stores and art galleries (which you probably won't be visiting with kids). It's fun to wander and look at everything.

Seventh Arrondissement

This is a fancy residential arrondissement. It has some terrific clothes and food shopping streets, but is not as easy to get around from by métro as some of the other arrondissements. There will also not be quite as many cafés around for alternative meals. The seventh is huge and spans out to include the Eiffel Tower and the Hôtel des Invalides (Napoleon's tomb and the Musée de L'Armée). Government buildings like the National Assembly are also here. I love the seventh, but I love it near the rue de Grenelle and rue de Bac areas, rather than near the Eiffel Tower. The Musée D'Orsay is in this arrondissement (in a great area) and is a definite must see.

Eighth Arrondissement

This elegant area includes many of the five-star hotels, as well as designer shops (avenue Montaigne) and pricey restaurants. Here you'll find the avenue des Champs-Elysées, which, to be honest, is commercial and a bit tacky. McDonald's and Hard Rock Cafe are both here. At Christmastime, though, the lights are beautiful. L'Arc de Triumph, Place de la Concorde and the Obelisk of Luxor (the oldest monument in Paris) are all here. Thomas Jefferson lived in this arrondissement at 20 rue de Berri when he was minister to France from 1785 to 1789. The building where he lived is no longer standing.

Ninth Arrondissement

Famous for the Opéra House and the Place Pigalle, this arrondissement also boasts the Folies Bergère. Shoppers can visit the department stores Printemps and Galleries Lafayette.

Tenth Arrondissement

This is not where you will be hanging out unless you are taking one of the trains at Gare du Nord or Gare de l'Est. This area is known for its strip joints.

Eleventh Arrondissement

The Opéra Bastille now stands in place of the original Bastille, and has done a bit to revive this area. It's becoming chic near the rue Oberkampf and the area around the new Opéra. Still, probably not a place you'll frequent.

Twelfth Arrondissment

If you visit this arrondissement, it will be most likely to go to the Bois de Vincennes, a huge, wonderful park that has an incredible zoo, lakes, a castle, and a gorgeous flower garden (Parc Floral de Paris). The aquarium is also here at the beginning of the park.

Thirteenth Arrondissement

Much of this area looks depressing, but it's nice where it meets the fifth arrondisement. This is Paris's Chinatown and home to the Gare d'Austerlitz.

Fourteenth Arrondissement

This area is known as Montparnasse and has some of the most famous literary cafés in Paris including La Coupole, La Dôme and Le Sélect. La Coupole is huge and beautiful, and while not exactly friendly, will make plain pasta for children.

Fifteenth Arrondissement

This is the largest arrondissement in Paris, beginning at Gare Montparnasse and winding to the Seine. It is mainly middle-class residential.

Sixteenth Arrondissement

A fancy and some maintain, snobbish area, which is largely residential. The sixteenth is large and incorporates a variety of fancy hotels and shops, as well as the Bois de Boulogne, which has the wonderful Jardin d'Acclimation.

Seventeenth Arrondissement

Interesting combination of affluent (western) and depressed neighborhoods (eastern). Two famous restaurants, Guy Savoy and Michel Rostang, are here, but I doubt you'll be dining there with your kids.

Eighteenth Arrondissement

Montmartre is here, although today the surrounding area is a conglomeration of tacky souvenir shops and bad, touristy restaurants. The Basilica of Sacré-Cœur, the Moulin Rouge and the Marché aux Puces de Clignancourt (huge flea market) are also in the 18th. Montmartre is the part of Paris that looks like the movie *GiGi*.

Nineteenth Arrondissement

You'll probably be taking the métro to the 19th for a visit to the fascinating Cité des Sciences et de L'Industrie (science center) and its adjacent park. Another great park, Buttes Chaumont, is also here.

Twentieth Arrondissement

This area is known for the Père-Lachaise cemetery (Jim Morrison, Edith Piaf, Isadora Duncan and many more). This is not the safest neighborhood, and I would not suggest wandering at night.

Paris is spliced by the Seine into two halves – north and south. The Left Bank is (literally) on the left. This bank (the Rive Gauche) is considered more relaxed than the Right Bank. The student quarter and the boulevard Saint-Germain are both here. The Right Bank is, of course, on the right, and has a bit more snob appeal because of shopping streets such as Avenue Montaigne and rue du Faubourg-St.-Honoré.

Hotels

Making room reservations:

It's important to understand that most hotel rooms in Paris are very small. They can seem doll-sized to Americans. This is just the way it goes. Your $150 to $400 a night will buy you a tiny room. Unless you stay at one of the Right-Bank legends – The Ritz, Bristol or Crillon – most quarters will not be opulent. They will, however, be charming and comfortable. Cots do not automatically come with a room. You will probably be charged a supplement between $20 and $100 per night. Most hotels will ask you to fax them a confirmation and a credit card number. Review their cancellation policy.

Our list of hotels includes child-friendly places with adjoining rooms. I also mention a few where side-by-side rooms can be booked if you have older children. These hotels do not have adjoining rooms, but only have a few rooms per floor. Some hotels with bigger rooms will let you have a child with you in the rooms (many free of charge). Many Parisian rooms, though, are just too small for that extra bed. Here are a few criteria I consider important.

- ✧ Comfort and charm – you should have a good time too.

- ✧ An English TV channel (don't laugh) like the Cartoon Network. There is no question that your kids will have some cultural overload and it helps to unwind with the familiar. They will need an hour or so each day, sprawled out on their beds.

✧   A nearby métro stop. Children get tired, and it can rain. You will be glad you stayed near a métro, the easiest and cheapest way to get around. There can be times when it's hard to get a cab. This is the only reason I didn't include some wonderful hotels on the Ile St.-Louis in my list.

✧   An accessible park. Paris is full of play areas for children.

✧   Air-conditioning.

Hotels: The absolute crème de la crème of the luxury hotels in Paris are the Crillon, Ritz, Bristol, Four Seasons, and Plaza Athénée. These hotels are so pricey that I haven't given descriptions. That doesn't mean that if you can afford it, you shouldn't stay at these hotels. It's just that most people can't. If you choose one of these, it will be wonderful but one of the most expensive things you've ever done. The Bristol in particular is very nice to children and has a pool.

I have concentrated on ease and charm, leaving many of the two-stars and out-of-the-way hotels out. The hotels in the book range greatly in price. Even the least expensive of these would please me, and that is not always easy. I've included current prices, but remember that they will most certainly change. Also prices can fluctuate seasonally and with promotions. Rooms go up and down like airfares, so make sure and check out a hotel that is appealing. It may be cheaper than you think.

When you are traveling with children, creature comforts count. You do not want to have to take them to a bathroom down the hall in the middle of the night, or be hot and cranky in the summer. It's also important to be in a convenient neighborhood. Here are a few more suggestions to make your trip easier.

Pick a hotel that serves breakfast late (most do) and – even better – is willing to bring it to your room. My kids, who are always up early, slept until 10:30 every morning. Everything in Paris is open until 7 p.m., so let them sleep. They will have a long day, and it's better not to have tired and cranky kids. Also remember that you probably will not eat until about 8 p.m., so they will be up late.

Choose a neighborhood that appeals to you. The Right Bank hotels are close to the fancy shops and what I call "crap" stores. These are souvenir shops, full of Paris wallets, T-shirts, Eiffel Tower miniatures and pencils your kids will love. There are areas of the Right Bank, such as the sixteenth arrondissement that are very residential, but the central areas in the first and the eighth arrondissements will have a more touristy, shopping kind of feel. Some of Paris's most elegant hotels are in these two arrondissements. The Left Bank has its share of fancy stores as well as little boutiques. It generally has a more casual feel. I'm a bit prejudiced, because I feel that this area is easier with children. You get more bang for your buck in the hotels; there are lots of small stores that sell fruit and drinks, and both the St. Sulpice area and the area surrounding Odéon are full of casual, child-friendly restaurants where you will not be expected to order a huge meal.

I always go immediately to buy water and snacks for our room. The supermarkets and Monoprix stores also sell disposable diapers (*couches à jeter*) and juice boxes (these are in the bottled and boxed juice – *jus des fruits* department), as well as small bottles of water to keep with you. Buy a few snacks to bring in your purse for those desperate moments. I bring zip-lock bags with me, so I can carry leftover bread or croissants from breakfast in our room. If you have older children, they can carry their own drinks in a backpack or a pocket.

Another option, if you have very young kids, or you don't want to deal with restaurant meals, is an apartment. There are a number of agencies that rent apartments that work well for families. The most well known is Chez Vous: 415-331-2535, which has well-located apartments. Its website is: www.ChezVous.com. Here you can view apartments and prices online.

Remember that Paris can be very hot in the summer. All the hotels in this book have air-conditioning, but the apartments probably won't. If this will bother you, it's something to think about. I hate to be hot.

Hotel prices are always subject to change, and many fluctuate wildly depending on occupancy. Be sure and check current prices before you reserve. Hotel staff can also turn over, and a wonderful front desk person could be replaced by a snippy one. I hope this doesn't happen – but there's always the chance.

First Arrondissement

Hotel Regina
2 place des Pyramides
75001 Paris
Métro: Palais Royal and Tuileries
Tel: 01-42-60-31-10
Fax: 01-40-15-95-16
Internet: www.Regina-hotel.com

This sedate, somewhat formal hotel faces the Tuileries and is walking distance to the Louvre, shops and the Musée d'Orsay. Its 120 rooms and suites (many have views of the Tuileries) are furnished with period furniture and have cable TV, soundproofed windows, and minibars. It also boasts a beautiful garden, an English bar, tearoom and the Pluvinel restaurant. A double room is 382 € to 440 €, and junior suites begin at 535 €. You may opt for a nonsmoking floor. The Regina has an English bar as well as a restaurant. Continental breakfast is 18 € per person, and a buffet breakfast is 26 € per person.
Nearest grocery store:
8 à Huit (eight to eight – like a 7-Eleven)
304 rue de Rivoli

Hôtel Intercontinental
3 rue de Castiglione
75001 Paris
Métro: Concorde or Tuileries
Tel: 01-44-77-11-11
Fax: 01-44-77-14-60
Toll free: 800-327-0200
Internet: www.interconti.com

This 450-room hotel has recently been completely renovated. The Intercontinental has a new fitness center and its large comfortable rooms have luxurious baths, minibars, and cable TV with pay TV movies, and Nintendo games, as well as nonsmoking areas. There is a restaurant, as well as room service. As you can see, this is a very large hotel, but the location is excellent. Room rates are listed as between 400 € and 860 € a room, but the Intercontinental frequently runs specials so it's worth checking if it appeals to you. Currently, if you reserve a room twenty-one days in advance with a nonrefundable deposit, a double including a rollaway is 313.06 €. There is another promotion for the same room with breakfast and no advance reservation or deposit for 350 €. One drawback is that connecting rooms are on request, which means they will not be confirmed until seven days before your trip. To accommodate a rollaway bed, you need a deluxe room, so be sure to mention if you need one. A continental breakfast is 17.53 € in the restaurant and 22.10 € in the room. An American breakfast is 25.15 € in the restaurant and 30 € in the room.

Nearest grocery store:
8 à Huit
304 rue de Rivoli

Hôtel de la Palace du Louvre
21 rue des Prêtres Saint-Germain-l'Auxerrois
75001 Paris
Métro: Louvre-Rivoli, Pont-Neuf
Tel: 01-42-33-78-68
Fax: 01-42-33-09-95

A small hotel in a fifteenth-century building on a tiny, quiet sidestreet near the Seine, and between the Louvre and the department store La Samaritaine. There are no connecting rooms, but there are only four rooms per floor, so it would be fine if you have older children. There is also one duplex that has a big bed downstairs and a twin in a loft upstairs. The hotel could add an extra bed, which would be a bit tight (no charge for a child under twelve). The stairs to the loft are steep, so I wouldn't consider this a good choice for young, mobile children. All the plain, but bright and pretty rooms have a TV set with foreign cable programs, minibar, private safe and hairdryer. A triple is 159 €. Buffet breakfast is 10 € per person and can be served either in your room or in the Musketeer's Cellar. Two double rooms next to each other with a view of the Louvre and the church Saint-Germain-L'Auxerrois are each

134 € a day, a duplex is 141 € and a triple is 150 €. There is a café with a crêpe stand on the corner.
Nearest grocery store:
There is a small grocery with fruit and drinks at 121 rue St. Honoré.

Second Arrondissement

Hôtel Westminster
13 rue de la Paix
75002 Paris
Métro: Opéra
Tel: 01-42-61-57-46
Fax: 01-42-60-30-66
Toll-free reservations: 800-203-3232
Internet: www.warwickhotels.com

The Westminster was built as a convent in 1846 and is conveniently located on a prime street between the Opéra and the Place Vendôme. It is owned by the Warwick chain and had a complete renovation in 1992. The 102 sumptuous rooms and suites are individually decorated with pretty fabrics and offer all the creature comforts: bathrobes, large, beautiful, marble bathrooms, satellite TV, minibars and safes. Each double room is 480 €, but there are frequent online promotions. Be sure to request adjoining rooms. A junior suite, which has a sitting room and couch, is 700 €. The Westminster also has a well-known, one-star Michelin restaurant, Le Céladon. Continental breakfast is 23 € per person and a buffet breakfast is 24 € per person.
Nearest grocery store:
Monoprix – the corner of rue de l'Opéra and rue des Pyramides

Hôtel Stendhal
22 rue Danielle Casanova
75002 Paris
Métro: Opéra
Tel: 01-44-58-52-52
Fax: 01-44-58-52-00

This small, fairly new (1992) hotel is located right near the Place Vendôme, and was once the home of the author Stendhal. The bedrooms have bright color schemes, and the bathrooms have red or blue sinks with navy-and-black abstract tile. The hotel's red-and-black suite honors Stendhal's famous novel, *The Red and the Black*. Each room has cable TV, minibar and generous closets. A double room is 264 € and superior suites begin at 297 €.

Nearest grocery store:
Monoprix – corner of rue de l'Opéra and rue des Pyramides

Hôtel Edouard VII
39 av. de l'Opéra
75002 Paris
Métro: Opéra
Tel: 01-42-61-56-90
Fax: 01-42-61-47-73
Internet: www.edouard7hotel.com

Edouard VII is a family-run, four-star hotel with seventy rooms and suites, each decorated differently with cheerful fabrics and furniture. All rooms have cable TV, minibar, safe, modem plugs, hairdryers, and soundproofing, and some higher ones view the Opéra. Double adjoining rooms are 297 € each, and breakfast is 20 € per person. It has a restaurant, as well as room service.

Nearest grocery store:
Monoprix – corner of rue de l'Opéra and rue des Pyramides

Third Arrondissement

Pavillon de la Reine
28 place des Vosges
75003 Paris
Métro: Bastille
Tel: 01-40-29-19-19
Fax: 01-40-29-19-20
Internet: www.pavillon-de-la-reine.com

Set on the most beautiful square in Paris, all the rooms in this special hotel face either the Place des Vosges or a flower-filled inner courtyard. While part of this hotel dates from the seventeenth century, the rest was a superb addition which looks as if it was always on the square. The 55 beautifully furnished rooms and suites are unique, but all have wooden beams, marble bathrooms and a luxurious feel. Double rooms are 365 €, deluxe doubles, 470 €, and junior suites are 520 €. There is room service and a continental breakfast is 20 €, while the buffet breakfast is 25 €.

Nearest grocery stores:
Tureene, 27 rue de Turenne (small)
Monoprix, 71 rue Sainte-Antoine or G-20 Supermarché, 115-117 rue Sainte-Antoine

Sixth Arrondissement

Note: Many of these hotels have the Buci marketplace listed as their nearest grocery store. Here, you'll find a supermarket (Champion) on the corner of rue de Buci and rue de Seine. Both of these streets are lined with fruit stands, flower stalls, cheese stores, butchers, *pâtisseries* and take-out gourmet *(traiteurs)*.

Hôtel de L'Abbaye
10 rue Cassette
75006 Paris
Métro: Saint-Sulpice
Tel: 01-45-44-38-11
Fax: 01-45-48-07-86
Internet: www.abbaye-paris-hotel.com

This cozy, forty-two–room, four-suite hotel was once an eighteenth-century convent. The first-floor rooms open to a small garden, and many of the top rooms have beamed ceilings and a lovely intimate feel. Service is kind and helpful, and breakfast (included in your room rate) may be served either in your room or the pretty bar room downstairs. In nice weather, you may eat outside. Adjoining rooms are available, and room prices begin at 206 € and vary, depending on size. The duplex suites are more expensive – 438 € – and can accommodate three. All have a safe, cable TV, and hairdryers.

Nearest grocery store:
Franprix on the corner of rue Cassette and rue de Rennes

Hôtel Relais Saint-Germain
9 Carrefour de l'Odéon
75006 Paris
Métro: Odéon
Tel: 01-43-29-12-05
Fax: 01-46-33-45-30

A tiny gem of a hotel with twenty-two rooms and suites decorated with lovely fabrics and furniture. All rooms have soundproofing, cable TV, radio, minibar, safe, and a marble bathroom with a hairdryer. The rates include breakfast, and doubles range from 285 € to 310 €. A duplex suite (350 €) features a deluxe room with a sofa and a sitting area, connected by a private stairway to a double bedroom with a private terrace. It has a nice, Parisian rooftop view, and a beautiful, beige-and-red marble bath. The hotel's restaurant, Comptoir du Relais, is a bistro/wine bar offering casual fare. It is next door and closed to the public for breakfast which is included, and may also be served in the room.

Nearest grocery store:
Buci Market – cut through the cobblestone walkway on bd. Saint-Germain (across the street from the Odéon métro station) to Saint-André-des-Arts and walk down toward rue Buci.

Restaurants nearby: A small, cobblestone walkway that leads from bd. Saint-Germain to rue Saint-André-des-Arts (across the street from the Odéon métro on bd. Saint-Germain) has lots of little restaurants, including some with children's menus that have hamburgers.

Premier Left Bank Saint Germain
9 rue de l'Ancienne Comédie
75006 Paris
Métro: Odéon

Tel: 01-43-54-01-70
Fax: 01-43-26-17-14
Toll-free to Best Western: 800-528-1234
Internet: www.bestwestern.com

Hôtel Left-Bank Saint Germain offers charm, space and value. In an excellent location, right near the Buci Market, this friendly thirty-room hotel is owned by Best Western. It's an excellent choice for three children, because there are large, twin bedrooms. The hotel is in a seventeenth-century building right next to Paris's oldest café, Café Procope. The richly colored, comfortable rooms have gorgeous, blood-red marble bathrooms. There are also adjoining rooms, but the number is limited so reserve ahead. All accommodations have cable TV, hairdryers, private safes and minibars. Breakfast is usually included and may be served in the breakfast room, or guests may fill out breakfast cards at night for room service delivery. Rates vary depending on the season, and Best Western often runs promotions. The average double room with a double bed is 216 €, and a room with twins is 216 € to 240 €. A triple averages 240 €.

Nearest grocery store:
Buci market is literally outside your door.

Hôtel Prince de Conti
8 rue Guénégaud
75006 Paris
Métro: Odéon, Saint-Michel or Pont-Neuf
Tel: 01-44-07-30-40
Fax: 01-44-07-36-34

Prince de Conti is in an eighteenth-century building on a quiet street near the Seine. Originally built for the Medeci family, it offers a fresh-looking English charm with its chintz-covered guestrooms, small, white marble bathrooms and an inviting drawing room. All twenty-six rooms and duplex suites have cable TV, minibars, soundproofing, hairdryers, and safes. There is also a nonsmoking floor. Some rooms open to a patio, where breakfast may be eaten in nice weather. One drawback is that the rooms are small and only have a minimal amount of storage space, about an 18" closet. The hotel has one set of adjoining rooms (on the third floor), so book well in advance if you need them. Otherwise, there are only four rooms per floor, so older kids would be fine. Room service is offered, and breakfast may be served in the room. Room rates vary but the current highest rate for a double is 218 €. One child under twelve may stay free with parents, but must pay for breakfast. The rooms are less expensive in July and August. The hotel sometimes offers winter promotional rates.

Nearest grocery store:
Buci Marketplace

Hôtel de Fleurie
32 rue Grégoire-de-Tours
75006 Paris
Métro: Odéon
Tel: 01-53-73-70-00
Fax: 01-53-70-70-20
Website: www.hotel-de-fleurie.tm.fr

A warm, friendly hotel run by the Marolleau family, Hôtel de Fleurie is an excellent location just off bd. St. Germain. The reception area is antique filled and the twenty-nine modern bedrooms are on the larger side, comfortably decorated in warm tones. While not fancy, this hotel is known for its family rooms and books up fast. These are called *chambres familiales* and are two rooms, sleeping a maximum of four. The children's room has a double bed and is small, but an extra bed could be added to the parents' room, if children do not want to share a bed. Family room prices range from 290 € to 325 €. All of Fleurie's rooms have cable TV, modem facilities, and minibar. The marble bathrooms are equipped with hairdryers and heated towel racks. Children under twelve may stay free on a cot in their parents' deluxe room (240 € to 265 €). An extra bed for a child over twelve is 25 €. A standard double room ranges from 165 € to 198 €, but will not accommodate an extra bed. Breakfast is 10 € and half-price for children under twelve. For a reservation of more than seven nights, the hotel offers a three-day museum pass.

Nearest grocery store:
Buci Marketplace – take the small, cobblestone walkway on bd. Saint-Germain (across from the Odéon métro station) and cut through to Saint-André-des-Arts and walk toward rue Buci.

Restaurants nearby: A small, cobblestone walkway that leads from bd. Saint-Germain to rue Saint-André-des-Arts (across the street from the Odéon métro on bd. St-Germain) has lots of little restaurants, including some with children's menus that have hamburgers.

Hôtel Lutetia
45 bd. Raspail
75006 Paris
Métro: Sèvres-Babylone
Tel: 01-49-54-46-46
Fax: 01-49-54-46-00
Toll free: 800-888-4747
Internet: www.lutetia-paris.com

You can't beat the Lutetia's location, and this hotel is used to accommodating families. An art deco hotel, the rooms are spacious and comfortable with cable TV, minibars, safes and hairdryers, and new, large bathrooms. The bathroom toiletries are all by Annick Goutal, a wonderful French perfume line. Deluxe rooms and suites have faxes. There is a merry-go-round with little cars right across the street, Bon Marché is down the block, and the restaurant Cherche Midi is right around the corner. This is a big hotel, 250 rooms and 30 suites. A tour bus unloaded, as I was walking through the lobby, and there was a convention as well as a bar mitzvah scheduled for that night. Although I'm not a fan of large hotels, I think Lutetia is an excellent choice for families – with its creature comforts and accommodating staff. A standard room is 290 € and a deluxe room is 381 €, suites are 686 € and up, and an extra bed is 92 €. Four people will fit in a suite. If you have three children, the hotel says that you would have to book two deluxe interconnecting rooms. The Lutetia frequently runs promotions that may include discounts on rooms and free breakfasts.

Nearest grocery store:
The Bon Marché food department, which is called Le Grande Épicerie, is down the block in its own building. It's huge and wonderful. There is a small fruit store, Espace Fruitier, at 46 rue du Cherche-Midi.

Less expensive breakfast: Cuisine de Bar, 8 rue Cherche-Midi

Hôtel Relais du Vieux Paris
9 rue git le Coeur
75006 Paris
Métro: Saint-Michel
Tel: 01-44-32-15-90
Fax: 01-43-26-00-15

What a history. This hotel was built in 1480 and belonged to the Duc de Luynes and the Duq d'O. In the 1950s and '60s the beat poets – Kerouac, Ginsberg, Corso and Burroughs hung out here. Today, this sophisticated hotel has thirteen rooms and seven suites decorated with Pierre Frey wallpaper and enchanting fabrics, exposed beams and white, marble bathrooms. Every room has cable TV, modem hook-up, safes, minibars, hairdryers and terrycloth robes. Double rooms with queen-sized beds are 207 € to 280 €, and children under twelve may stay free in their parents' room. The hotel can also provide a crib and stroller. Three suites have a sitting room with a sofa bed, and a bedroom with a queen-sized bed, as well as Jacuzzis. They are 307 € to 350 €. There are also some twin-bedded suites with a balcony and rooftop views. The only drawback to this hotel is the steep and narrow stairs. They are dangerous for kids, and I'd advise taking the tiny elevator in shifts. Breakfast is in the cozy, red paisley breakfast room and includes fresh orange juice, croissants, butter, jam, cheese, cake, coffee, Earl Gray tea, hot chocolate, and fruit salad. It is 13 €.

Nearest grocery store:
Buci Marketplace.

Restaurants: Lots of casual choices nearby on rue Saint-André-des-Arts and on rue de la Huchette in the student quarter.

Seventh Arrondissement

Hôtel Le Tourville
16 av. Tourville
75007 Paris
Métro: Ecole Militaire
Tel: 01-47-05-43-90
Fax: 01-47-05-43-90

This light and lovely, thirty-room hotel decorated by David Hicks is located between the Dôme des Invalides, the Rodin Museum and the Eiffel Tower. The Champ-de-Mars park, which has a playground with basketball hoops and a merry-go-round is across the street. Le Tourville has three junior suites accommodating four (or five with a rollaway bed). However, while the junior suites were charming with a skylight and rooftop view (from the attic suite), they are one big room, so there is absolutely no privacy. The double rooms – which are not connected, but next to each other – might be a better option with older kids. The softly colored rooms are golden yellow, sand or pink, and have airy-looking white spreads, soundproofing, cable TV and hairdryers. The black-and-white bathrooms are perfectly fine, but not luxurious. A junior suite is 310 €, and the rooms are 145 € to 240 € (the more expensive ones have a terrace). Breakfast is 12 €.

Nearest grocery store:
Supermarché Shopi
42 av. La Motte Picquet – this is across the street from the métro station and around the corner from the hotel.

Hôtel Montalembert
3 rue Montelembert
75007 Paris
Métro: Rue de Bac
Tel: 01-45-49-68-68
Fax: 01-45-49-69-49
Internet: www.montalembert.com

This trendy, sleek hotel looks like the kind of place that might not welcome children, but they love them. All the rooms have VCRs, and the hotel maintains a collection of children's movies, so you don't have to search for rentals. This is probably the most luxurious hotel on the Left Bank – and it doesn't come cheap. The small rooms were designed by design guru Grace Leo Andrieu and have huge towels, robes, Frette sheets and glamorous marble. All rooms have cable TV, minibar and safe. The hotel also has an excellent dining room and twenty-four-hour room service. Each double room is 340 € to 430 € and breakfast is 20 € per person. Cots may be added to deluxe rooms, and one-bedroom suites sleep four.

Nearest grocery store:
Proxi
24 rue de Bac

Eighth Arrondissement

Lancaster
7 rue de Berri
75008 Paris
Métro: Georges V
Tel: 01-40-76-40-76
Fax: 01-40-76-40-00
Internet: www.hotel-lancaster.fr/eng/around_eng.htm (great Paris links)

Smack in the middle of fast-food restaurants and tacky stores, the Lancaster is an elegant surprise. It's built around a courtyard garden where clematis and roses wind up the walls in the summer, and the spare lobby is decorated with an exceptional collection of French antiques juxtaposed with sleek modern pieces. Each gorgeous room is equipped with cable TV, VCR, safes, and minibars. Paintings by Russian painter Boris Patoukhoff are all over the hotel as he paid for his room and board here with his work. A standard room is 400 € and may be connected to a superior (450 €) or deluxe (500 €) room. The deluxe double rooms may have either a king or twins, and it's possible to add an extra bed to this room, but not to a standard or a superior. Breakfast is 28 € per person. This is a very quiet hotel and the large rooms connect in a way that seems very private. The staff is exceptional and welcomes children. Twenty-four-hour room service is offered and there is a fitness center with a sauna. The Chicago Pizza Kitchen is on the same block.

Nearest grocery store:
Prisunic Exploitation
52 av. des Champs-Elysées (the corner of rue Boétie and av. des Champs-Elysées). Food is in the basement.

Hyatt Regency Paris-Madeline
24 bd. Malesherbes
750008 Paris
Métro: Madeline
Tel: 01-55-27-12-34
Fax: 01-55-27-12-35
Toll free: 800-633-7313
Internet: www.Hyatt.com

This was the Hyatt's first venture into Paris (its other hotel is at the airport), and it did a wonderful job. Hyatt has since opened a new deluxe hotel – Park Hyatt Vêndome. The Hyatt Madeline is an eighty-six–room hotel perfectly located near the fancy shops and Place Madeline. The lobby is built around a glass dome from 1901 that creates a sense of history in this more modern hotel. The rooms are sleek and comfortable at the same time. There are soft pillows and fluffy quilts on the beds, and the marble bathrooms are quite large. All rooms have cable TV, desks, safes, robes, hairdryers, faxes and modems. There is also a fitness center right in the hotel. Rooms range from 330 € to 460 € and the staff is friendly and helpful. Check for Hyatt specials and discounts.

Nearest grocery store:
Monoprix
47 bd. Malesherbes
Alternative breakfast: Laudurée, 16 rue Royale

Hôtel San Regis
12 rue Jean-Goujon
75008 Paris
Métro: Alma-Marceau
Tel: 01-44-95-16-16
Fax: 01-45-61-05-48
Internet: www.hotel-sanregis.fr

The San Regis radiates a quiet elegance with its sophisticated blend of antiques and modern amenities. Tucked away on a street right near the Avenue Montaigne, this forty-four–room hotel has a restaurant, room service and all the creature comforts. The rooms and marble baths are spacious and beautiful, with fabrics matching the period furniture. Double rooms are 395 € and breakfast is 20 per person. There are also junior suites at 590 € and full suites are 1025 €. The San Regis is very quiet and private, and has the feeling of a luxurious home. Continental breakfast is 20 €.

Nearest grocery store:
Supermarché Elysées
12 rue Tremoille (This is a few blocks away.)

Hôtel Amarante Beau Manoir
6 rue de l'Arcade
75008 Paris
Métro: Madeline
Tel: 01-53-43-28-28
Fax: 01-53-43-28-88
Website: info@hotelbeaumanoir.com

This is a delightful four-star hotel right near the Madeline church. Its Louis XIII-style rooms are small, but charming, decorated with French country furniture. In many rooms, the bed is a double, which may be smaller than you are accustomed to sleeping in at home. The bathrooms are a striking red marble. Each room has small cable TV, a minibar, safe, soundproofing and a hairdryer. A double room is between 275 € and 285 €. Two rooms may be connected

by a small hallway and shut off by a main common door like an apartment.
Nearest grocery store:
Monoprix
47 bd. Malesherbes

Sixteenth Arrondissement

Hôtel le Parc
55-57 av. Raymond Poincaré
75116 Paris
Métro: Trocadéro or Victor Hugo
Tel: 01-44-05-66-66
Fax: 01-44-05-66-00
Internet: www.pariserve.com/le-parc/english.htm

Nina Campbell decorated the lush rooms at Le Parc with chintz flower prints, canopy beds and sumptuous bathrooms. The hotel has a beautiful courtyard garden where guests can eat breakfast in the summer. Some of the rooms have a garden view. There is also a library, bar and health club. While Le Parc is elegant, it has a very relaxed feel and a nice staff. Chef Alain Ducasse's restaurant is in the hotel and is wonderful. A superior room is 450 €-480 € and may be connected with a deluxe room which is 550 €. A junior suite is 620 €. Breakfast is 26 € per person. There is a Häagen-Dazs ice cream store down the street.
Nearest grocery store:
Alimentation GLE
101 Lauriston

St. James Club Paris
43 av. Bugeaud
75015 Paris
Métro: Porte Dauphin
Tel: 01-44-05-81-81
Fax: 01-44-05-81-82
Toll free: 800-233-5652 and 233-5652

This hotel is a small château built in 1892 to accommodate gifted scholars studying in Paris, and was restored in 1992 to its original splendor. Set in a walled garden, the St. James Club is actually a private dining and health club with a library full of leather-bound books and inviting chairs. Guests have access to all the facilities. All forty-eight rooms are decorated in soft, pretty colors and antiques and have cable TV, mini-bars, beautiful bathrooms, hairdryers and safes. There is a restaurant, which is the private dining room, but it is closed on weekends. Room service is available. There are only four connecting rooms in the hotel, so book well in advance if you're counting on them. Double rooms range from 335 € to 420 €, and suites are 700 €. The hotel also takes dogs, but specifies only nice ones.

Nearest grocery stores:
Super A3 AZ
55 av. Bugeaud
Au Bon Accueil
30 av. Bugeaud

Restaurants

I use my museum method for taking children to dinner in Paris (one museum, then one park). One pasta night for you; one bistro night for me. My boys have grown to enjoy bistros, but they still love their pizza and pasta. And, as much as I hate to say it, Italians don't have as many etiquette rules, so you can let your guard down a bit. Alternating gives everyone a break, and still lets you enjoy wonderful food every night.

There are several restaurants in Paris (mainly chains) that are geared towards families and have children's menus. Most Parisian kids' menus have either a steak *haché* (hamburger without a bun), a regular hamburger or chicken. The meals usually come with a drink or dessert, and they often have diversions such as crayons. The most well-known chains are Hippopotamus and Bistro Romaine. To be honest, my children don't particularly like hamburgers, but these places are a good alternative, especially with little ones. The chain my boys do like is Leon's of Brussels, which is the best deal in town with kids – there's a children's portion of mussels and fries on the menu. Pizza is also always a safe choice with picky eaters.

On the other hand, if it's not too stressful, go out and have great meals. It will open up a new world for your children – my seven-year-old discovered sole meunière is his favorite food. With a little help, most children can find something they like on any menu. I believe that love of good food is a great gift to give children. You can have a hamburger anywhere. So, unless you have toddlers you'd have to chase around a restaurant, go out and enjoy.

Kids:

Bistro Romain

This bistro has tons of locations and offers a 7.50 € kids' menu of chicken croquettes, hamburgers, lasagna, fries or pasta, ice cream, crème caramel or chocolate mousse and unlimited drinks. I'll list two of its popular restaurants.

>103 bd. de Montparnasse
>75006 Paris
>Tel: 01-43-25-25 25
>Métro: Edgar Quinet or Montparnasse

>122 av. des Champs-Elysées
>75008 Paris
>Tel: 01-45-61-01-73
>Métro: Georges V

Hippopotamus

Known for its hamburgers and steak *tartare*, Hippo also has veggie burgers, salmon, chicken, and salads. The children's 7.17 €

menu is a choice of a Hippo burger, chicken or lamb chops (all with matchstick potatoes), a salad, and a dessert of either chocolate mousse, ice pop or yogurt. Once again, there are many locations, but I'll list just two.

> 119 bd. Montparnasse
> 75006 Paris
> Tel: 01-43-20-37-04
> Métro: Vavin

> 42 av. des Champs-Elysées
> 75008 Paris
> Tel: 01-53-83-94-50
> Métro: Franklin Roosevelt

Chicago Pizza Pie Factory
5 rue Berri
75008 Paris
Tel: 01-45-62-50-23
Métro: Georges V

I'm from Chicago and my kids live on pizza, so I'm judgmental. It's good here – the deep-dish kind. The restaurant is noisy and fun, and a birthday party spot for French children. It's a nice break from a three-course meal. My crew was happy to kick back and color the menu. Saturday and Sunday lunch between 1 and 2 p.m. is kids' hour with clowns, magicians and more. The children's menu of 8.53 € is available all week and includes mushroom or ham pizza or chicken legs, fries, ice cream and unlimited Coke, lemonade or orange soda.

Léon de Bruxelles
Once again, Leon's is all over Paris, so I'll just list two. This is the Belgian mussels and fries place – and quite good. It has mussels prepared in many different ways, some salads, and ice cream and waffle desserts. The children's menu includes a choice of mussels or a bunless hamburger, fries, a drink, and a dessert of chocolate mousse or ice cream. Kids may

take their menus home and get them stamped for gifts on consecutive visits. There are also lollipops.

>131 bd. Saint-Germain
>75006 Paris (corner of rue de Rennes and bd. Saint-Germain)
>Tel: 01-43-26-45-95
>Métro: Saint-Germain, Mabillon, Odéon

>63 av. des Champs-Elysées
>75008 Paris
>Tel: 01-42-25-96-16
>Métro: Georges V
>(This has outdoor tables in the summer.)

Adult restaurants with children's menus:

Le Cap Vernet
82 av. Marceau
75008 Paris
Tel: 01-47-20-20-40
Métro: Charles de Gaulle-Etoile
Open: Every day
Hours: Lunch is from 12 to 2:30 p.m. and dinner is from 7 to midnight.

This Guy Savoy bistro is well known for its excellent seafood and offers a children's menu, called "*Découverte-des-Saveurs*" (discover the flavors) for Saturday and Sunday lunch. The menu changes with the seasons and is definitely gourmet with dishes such as salmon, mussels, and lamb. Desserts which win high approval have included fruit tarts and chocolate fondant. The adult lunch menu ranges from 23 € to 30.50 €. It's a great way to introduce children to nicer restaurants and French food.

La Butte Chaillot
110 av. Kléber
75016 Paris

Tel: 01-47-27-88-88
Métro: Trocadéro
Open: Every day
Hours: Lunch is served from 12 to 2:30 p.m. and dinner is from 7 to midnight. Saturday – closed for lunch.

Another Guy Savoy bistro that features monthly specialties from a different region in France. The set menu is 30 € and includes a first course, second course, and dessert. Some favorites include roast chicken with mashed potatoes and a multicolored salad with crunchy sesame-crusted prawns. While they have no special children's menu, they say they're happy to prepare a kid-friendly plate.

My Favorites Bistros:

The French rarely take their children out for dinner. So, you'll just have to get over the fact that there are no other children in the restaurant. These places are good for reasonably behaved kids who can sit through a dinner. My goal was wonderful food and low prices in a casual atmosphere. A few are more expensive, but this is noted in the descriptions. Play it safe and make reservations, as all of the restaurants are small. I've mentioned those which are open on Sunday, which is always a problem in Paris. Many restaurants are even closed on Saturday night. If you will be in Paris during the summer, especially August, call to check if the restaurant is open. Many close for vacation.

When you are at a restaurant, you are expected to eat a meal. It's not all right to order soup or salad, as you might at home. The waiter is not trying to be rude about bringing water to the table. The French generally drink bottled water (and wine) at dinner. You can always ask for tap water. It's perfectly fine.

Coffee after breakfast is always an espresso. It's never drunk with dinner or dessert, and it will be brought black, unless you ask for it with milk (which is considered inappropriate with dinner).

The tip or service is 15 percent, and is included in the bill. For attentive service, it's always nice to leave a little extra – although it's not expected.

L'Appart
9 rue du Colisée
75008 Paris
Tel: 01-53-75-42-00
Métro: Franklin D. Roosevelt
Open: Every day
Hours: Lunch is from 12 to 2:30 p.m. and dinner is from 7:30 to midnight.

This trendy restaurant is in a great location right off the Champs-Elysées. The food is good and L'Appart has a warm feeling with its polished floors and Oriental rugs, although it's actually quite big. There is a fixed price 30 € menu, which features two choices per course. With kids, you may have to order a la carte, which is also fairly reasonable. There are homey choices such as chicken and steak, and large delicious green salads. Cheese ravioli is sure to please pasta eaters.

Le Bamboche
15 rue Babylone
Paris 75007
Tel: 01-45-49-14-40
Métro: Sèvres-Babylone
Open: Monday through Friday

While this is not a restaurant I would normally recommend for children, I have to because the owners are so warm and wonderful. Le Bamboche is small with eight tables, and the food is sophisticated. So, it is for children who are a bit older and adventurous. One of Bamboche's well-known starters is oyster ice cream. While it's not my favorite, I know several children who are still talking about it. All the main courses are great, as are the desserts. The bill averages about 57 € a person.

Au Bascou
38 rue Réamur
75003 Paris

Tel: 01-42-72-69-25
Métro: Arts et Métiers
Open: Monday through Saturday for dinner, and Monday through Friday for lunch.
Hours: 12 to 2 p.m. for lunch, and 8 to 10:30 p.m. for dinner

Besides having the coolest bathroom in Paris, Au Bascou has some of the best food. This, combined with friendly service, makes it one of my top picks. There is no set menu here, and prices run about 35 € per person. The restaurant features Basque specialties that included a delicious omelet and red peppers stuffed with salt cod as starters when we visited. There was also a fantastic asparagus soup. The main course, salmon, was one of the most wonderful I've ever had, and we all left happy.

Baracane
38 rue des Tournelles
75004 Paris
Tel: 01-42-71-43-33
Métro: Bastille
Open: Monday through Friday for lunch and dinner. On Saturday, it's open just for dinner.
Hours: Lunch is 12 to 2:30 p.m. and dinner is 7 p.m. to midnight

Delicious food and reasonable prices combined with kind service makes this restaurant, specializing in food from southwest France, a good choice. The fixed-price dinner menu of 35 € has generous portions of hearty food. The olives on the table were a big hit and the beef *bourguignonne* was devoured. There was even a spinach and cheese vegetarian dish on the menu. Baracane has a delicious leek terrine and; of course, wonderful chocolate cake for dessert. You have to go out the backdoor and through a tiny courtyard backing up to the kitchen to get to the bathroom, so you might want to accompany small children. My little one had trouble with the door.

Au Bon Acceuil
14 rue de Monttessuy

75007 Paris
Tel: 01-47-05-46-11
Métro: Alma-Marceau
Open: Monday through Friday
Hours: Lunch is 12 to 2:30 p.m. and dinner is 7:30 to 10:15 p.m.

When you walk through the door of Au Bon Acceuil, you feel as if you're eating right under the Eiffel Tower. The food here is very good and the service is sweet. There is a set dinner menu of 29 €, but it is easy to be tempted by the a la carte menu. The night we visited there was a fantastic sole and a warm chocolate cake with a liquid interior that the waiter made sure my kids ordered for dessert. He was right.

La Bastide d'Odéon
7 rue Corneille
75006 Paris
Tel: 01-43-26-03-65
Métro: Odéon
Open: Tuesday through Saturday
Hours: Lunch is 12:30 to 2 p.m. and dinner is 7:30 to 11:00 p.m.

The restaurant closes over holidays and for vacation in the summer. Call to check. Quiet and pretty, with delicious food, this restaurant is on the slightly more expensive side. My children continue to talk about this place. We had chestnut soup, marinated eggplant, snapper, and steak. The set menu was 30.25 €, but there was also a la carte. The waiter was very sweet and my family loved the food,

Le Bistro Papillon
6 rue Papillon
75009 Paris
Tel: 01-47-70-90-03
Métro: Cadet or Poissonnière
Open: Monday through Friday
Hours: Lunch is 12 to 2 p.m. and dinner is 7 to 10 p.m.

In the Montmartre district, this is a classic neighborhood bistro with fish, duck, and steak. It is a little hidden gem featuring traditional French dishes. When I asked if two of my children could share a steak, they brought them each a small one with fries. My boys inhaled an appetizer of risotto and shrimp so fast we had to order an extra one. Service was efficient and kind. Cost of an adult meal averages about 38 €.

Bistro de la Grille
1 rue Guisarde
75006 Paris
Tel: 01-43-54-16-87
Métro: Mabillon
Open: Every day
Hours: Lunch is from 12 to 3:30 p.m. and dinner is from 7 p.m. to 12:30 a.m.

This bustling bistro, decorated with old photos of film stars, has decent food and cheerful service. In the summer, outside tables are set up on the sidewalk, but be sure to reserve one in advance. The 24.30 € price-fixed menu has a lot of variety. We had a tasty special of crab soup and salmon. Bistro de la Grille is also open on Sunday – a plus. It's also a very convenient location if you are staying on the Left Bank.

Les Bookinistes
53 quai des Grands Augustins
75006 Paris
Tel: 01-43-25-45-94
Fax: 01-43-25-23-07
Métro: Saint-Michel or Pont-Neuf
Open: Every day, but closed Saturday and Sunday for lunch.
Hours: Lunch is served from noon until 2 p.m. and dinner from 7 p.m. to midnight.

Guy Savoy strikes again with this elegant, lively bistro facing the Seine. The staff was brave enough to put us in a front window, and was willing to mix orange juice and Perrier for an impromptu Orangina.

The food is delicious and reasonably priced with classic dishes such as sole and steak. An adult meal will average close to 50 €.

Chez Diane
25 rue Servandoni
75006 Paris
Tel: 01-46-33-12-06
Métro: St. Sulpice
Open: Every day
Hours: Monday through Saturday, lunch is served from 12 to 2:30 p.m. and dinner is served Monday through Friday from 7 p.m. to 12:30 a.m. On Sunday dinner is the only meal served and service stops at 11 p.m.

This tiny, pretty restaurant is right across from the Luxembourg Gardens and has a 35 € fixed-price meal. You also have the option of ordering a la carte. Two of my children tried duck for the first time, and loved it. This bistro is welcoming and an easy walk from many Left Bank hotels.

Chez Marianne
2 rue des Hospitaliers Saint Gervais
75004 Paris
Tel: 01-42-72-18-86
Métro: Saint-Paul
Open: Every day
Hours: Continuous

This tiny, Middle-Eastern restaurant is packed, so book ahead. It's wonderful for kids, because you can choose how much and what you want from a menu with a wide variety of specialties. I sat next to a fourteen-month-old baby here, and ordered five dishes, which is plenty for an adult. The eggplant dishes are excellent – *babbaganoush* and fried eggplant with tomato. There is *hummus, dolmas* and a Middle Eastern meatball. Cheesecake, poppy seed cake, and fruit tarts are served for dessert. The food is plentiful and inexpensive. The most you could spend for an adult would be about 25 €.

La Cafétèria
21 rue Mazarine
75006 Paris
Tel: 01-46-33-76-90
Métro: Odéon or St.-Germain-des-Pres
Open: Tuesday through Saturday
Hours: 7:30 to 11:00 p.m. (11:30 Friday and Saturday)

This homey restaurant is decorated with antique coffee pots and offers food that's sure to please all. The menu is actually Italian, so there's plenty of pasta to choose from, as well as salads and fish. The service is warm, which makes for a relaxing dinner. My children adore this place. An average adult meal is about 42 €, but the children don't need to order three courses here, if they don't want a full meal.

La Cônnivence
1 rue de Cotte
75012 Paris
Tel: 01-46-28-46-17
Open: Every day
Métro: Ledru-Rollin or Gare de Lyon
Hours: Lunch is served from 12 to 2 p.m. and dinner is served from 7:45 to 11 p.m.

This somewhat out-of-the-way spot has excellent food and the prices are incredibly low. The menu changes every two months. When we visited there was a wonderful excellent vegetable soup, a brioche shell with leeks and cashew nuts, salmon with sweet corn and tarragon, duck leg with sangria sauce and a puree of broccoli *rabe*, an apple and chestnut tart, rum baba and a chocolate cake with pine nuts and hazelnut. Currently the restaurant offers two menus – one 23 € and the other 30 €.

Cherche Midi
22 rue du Cherche Midi
75006 Paris

Tel: 01-45-48-27-44
Métro: Sèvres-Babylone
Open: Every day
Hours: Lunch is 12 to 3 p.m. and dinner is 8 to 11:30 p.m.
Métro: Sèvres Babylone or Saint Sulpice

Classic Italian. We had an arugula salad, grilled shrimp and pasta. The food is good, and kids love pasta. It is, however, a bit expensive, and I wouldn't call them warm and friendly. However, you can't beat the location if you're staying at the Lutetia. Please note that credit cards are not accepted, and the bill averages about 40 € per person.

Chez Catherine
3 rue Berryer
75008 Paris
Tel: 01-40-76-01-40
Métro: Georges V
Closed on Saturday, Sunday and *Monday evenings*

My new favorite restaurant, which is better to visit with slightly older kids as it's very small. The menu changes with the seasons, and we had fantastic scallops and a pear tart when we were here. The wine list is carefully chosen with well-priced selections. An average meal would run about 65 € per person, and because it's so small you need to reserve well in advance.

Chez Fabrice
38 rue Crois des Petit Champs
75001 Paris
Tel: 01-40-20-06-46
Métro: Palais Royale
Open: Monday through Friday
Hours: Monday through Friday lunch is served, on Saturday only dinner.

Chez Fabrice offers delicious dishes such as a small casserole of scallops and mussels in a saffron cream sauce, a filet of Sandre (like perch) on a bed of *ratatouille*, a boneless guinea fowl breast cooked with prunes and served with mashed potatoes, a warm pear *clafouti*, and pistachio profiteroles with chocolate sauce. The cost averages about 35 € a person.

La Coupole
102 bd. du Montparnasse
75014 Paris
Tel: 01-43-20-14-20
Métro: Vavin
Open: Every day but the night of December 24
Hours: Lunch is served 12 to 3 p.m. and dinner is served from 7 p.m. to 1:30 a.m.

Huge and a bit like a production line, but a beautiful room. The host rolled his eyes (not kindly) when we walked in with five boys, but the service was patient. They even made plain pasta, which was not on the menu, for the kids. You can definitely do better for your money at any of the smaller bistros, but this historical place is open when others are closed. We ate here on Christmas, because it was open and it's fine in a pinch. Cost averages about 45 € per person.

Da Alfredo Positano
9 rue Guisarde
75006 Paris
Tel: 01-43-26-90-52
Métro: St-Sulpice
Closed on Sunday

This casual Italian restaurant has good everything. It's also often full of kids, especially on the weekend. A dazzling antipasti spread greets you as you enter, and the menu offers pasta, pizza, fish, and meats. Ask about daily specials. They're usually amazing.

L'Epi Dupin
11 rue Dupin
75006 Paris
Tel: 01-42-22-64-56
Métro: Sèvres-Babylone
Open: Monday through Saturday
Hours: Lunch is served Tuesday through Friday noon to 2 p.m. Dinner is served 7:30 to 11 p.m.

Energetic and bustling, L'Epi Dupin serves a 29.80 € fixed-price menu with a Mediterranean flavor. The food is terrific, so this small place is packed all the time. However, unless you have sophisticated eaters, this might be a better "date" night choice. The menu changes, and there is not a staple like roast chicken offered. While the staff was accommodating, and prepared an artichoke salad without duck hearts, the most kid-friendly dish on the menu was quail. Needless to say, this did not go over big. Be sure to reserve more than two weeks in advance here, and note that there are a few outdoor sidewalk tables in the summer.

Au Moulin a Vent "Chez Henri"
20 rue des Fosses St. Bernard
75005 Paris
Métro: Jussieu
Tel: 01-43-54-99-37
Open: Tuesday through Saturday
Hours: Lunch is served from 12:30 to 2 p.m. and dinner is 7:30 to 10:15 p.m.

This has the feel of a neighborhood bistro, with its tightly packed tables and garlicky aroma. It's fantastic for steaks, which are prepared all different ways. There was no main course of fish on the menu when we were here, so being a meat lover is essential. Occasionally, there are fish specials. The side order of mushrooms was fantastic. Our meals averaged 62 € apiece.

L'Oeillade
10 rue de Saint-Simon
75007 Paris
Tel: 01-42-22-01-60
Métro: rue de Bac or Solferino
Open: Monday through Saturday
Hours: Lunch is served Monday through Friday from 12:30 to 2 p.m. and dinner is served Monday through Saturday 7:30 to 11 p.m.

Oeillade's 26.70 € fixed-price menu is packed with just the kind of dishes you want to order. It changes daily, but there's always wonderful comfort food – a steaming bowl of mussels, roast chicken, grilled fish. The staff is patient even though the restaurant is crowded with people enjoying its excellent food and reasonable prices.

La Rôtisserie d'en Face
2 rue Christine
75006 Paris
Tel: 01-43-26-40-98
Métro: Odéon or Saint-Michel
Open: Monday through Saturday
Hours: Monday through Friday lunch is served from 12:30 to 2 p.m. and Monday through Saturday dinner is 7 to 10 p.m.

A Jacques Cagna bistro, facing his famous high-priced restaurant across the street. This is your chance to sample his wonderful whole grain bread from across the street. The bistro has a 39 € fixed menu which is available in English or French, so bring kids who eat. There are a lot of Americans here, and the service can be a bit hyper, but the food is delicious. The bistro menu features grilled and spit-roasted meats – the roast chicken with mashed potatoes is excellent. There are also always some fish dishes such as salmon and scallops.

La Régalade
49 av. Jean-Moulin

75014 Paris
Tel: 01-45-45-68-58
Métro: Alésia
Open: Tuesday through Saturday
Hours: Tuesday through Friday lunch is served from 12 to 3 p.m. and Tuesday through Saturday dinner is 7:30 to midnight.

The food here is outstanding, and the whole world knows it, so reserve at least a month in advance. La Régalade has a 30 € fixed-price menu that changes seasonally, but my children had no trouble finding dishes they wanted to eat, including scallops with pesto and chestnut soup. The service is a bit serious. It's hard to get them to crack a smile, but the food is worth it. Go.

Le Soufflé
36 rue du Mont-Thabor
75001 Paris
Tel: 01-42-60-27-19
Métro: Concorde
Open: Monday through Saturday
Hours: Lunch is 12 to 2:30 p.m. and dinner is 7 to 10:30 p.m.

While this is definitely a touristy restaurant, the service is nice and the food is terrific. For 30 €, you can have three soufflés, an appetizer, main course and dessert. We had cheese, mushroom, chocolate and raspberry. They were perfect. There is also a nice reasonably priced a la carte menu with dishes like onion soup and steak, in addition to the soufflés.

Stresa
7 rue Chambiges
75008 Paris
Métro: Alma Marceau
Tel: 01-47-23-51-62
Open: Monday through Friday, Saturday for lunch only.

Hours: until 10:30 p.m.
Closed December 20 to January 3.

Very chic and Italian, Stresa is the place to go for an arugula salad and a perfectly cooked plate of pasta. It's not cheap. Dinner for four was 244 € with tax and tip, but the people-watching was worth it. The food's wonderful and the service is kind. There is even plain pasta with tomato sauce on the menu.

Les Olivades
41 av. de Ségur
75007 Paris
Tel: 01-47-83-70-09
Métro: Ecole Militaire or Ségur
Open: Tuesday through Saturday
Hours: Lunch is served Tuesday through Friday and only dinner is served Saturday. It's open until 10:30 p.m.

This provincial restaurant is a happy, pretty place with excellent food and a kind staff. They had no problem whipping up a vegetarian platter for my son, and we were all happy.

Le Vieux Bistro
14 rue du Cloître-Nôtre-Dame
75004 Paris
Tel: 01-43-54-18-95
Métro: Cité
Open: Every day except December 24 and 25
Hours: Lunch is served from 12 to 2 p.m. and dinner is 7 to 10:30 p.m.

Trapped between souvenir stores across from Nôtre Dame, you will think you've made a terrible mistake when you arrive at Le Vieux Bistro. Open the door and enter a classic French bistro with top-notch food. This was probably the place the vegetarians had the most trouble. The only thing offered was a potato gratin (they wolfed it down), but they made up for this with desserts. The rest of us were happy with delicious sole meunière, scallops, and filet mignon. The bill was close to 50 € a person, but the restaurant is open Sunday night. Be sure to reserve ahead.

France 101

Your children will enjoy Paris more if they know a little of its history. A quick and painless way to do this is at Paristoric. It's fun – historically pertinent people and moments are shown on a screen, while dramatic music plays in the background. The history is delivered via headphones in English, and the whole show is about forty-five minutes.

Paristoric
11 bis rue Scribe
75009 Paris
Tel: 01-42-66-62-06
Métro: Opéra, Havre Caumartin
Hours: In summer it's open every day from 9 a.m. to 9 p.m., and in winter it's open from 9 a.m. to 6 p.m. daily.
Admission – Adults: 8 €, Children: 5 € (under six: free)

A Very Brief French History

The most interesting part of French history for kids will, of course, be the revolution and Napoleon. Linking the history with the sites will make it more memorable.

Paris was first settled at the end of the third century on the Ile de la Cité by the Gallic Parisii tribe who called it Lutetia (like the hotel). This is also where Nôtre Dame is, but the church wasn't built until the twelfth century. Another church, and possibly two, occupied its site.

In 52 BC, Julius Caesar conquered Paris. This was during the Gallic War. Paris became a Roman town for the next four hundred years. During this time, Paris expanded to what is now the Left Bank.

About 1100, Paris became a leading city and the Sorbonne University was founded on the Left Bank. This attracted intellectuals, and Paris became known for its scholars. In 1167, Les Halles food market began on the Right Bank. In 1348, the plague – Black Death – infested Paris.

In 1422, France was invaded by England during the Hundred Years War. England captured parts of France. In 1429, Joan of Arc led a movement against the English and was burned at the stake in 1431. France defeated the English in 1453.

In 1500, Francois I was crowned the first Renaissance king. This was the beginning of much of the building still seen today in Paris. Catherine de Medici commissioned the Tuileries Palace for herself, and the Louvre underwent tremendous expansion. From this period until the revolution, the kings and queens constructed many palaces. Marie de Médici, the widow of Henry IV, built the Luxembourg palace and gardens (the French senate now meets in the palace). The Palais Royal was created for Louis XIII (by orders of Cardinal Richelieu as the king was a boy too young to rule). Louis XIV, who was known as the "sun king," built himself Versailles Palace, outside of Paris, as it was thought the city was an unhealthy place to live.

Versailles was the last hurrah for the monarchy as the French people revolted on July 14, 1789, beginning the French Revolution. On that day an enormous, angry mob broke into the prison called the Bastille, freeing the prisoners – and killing the prison head. The prison was destroyed. The Opéra Bastille now stands on its site. In August 1792, troops captured King Louis XVI and his queen, Marie Antoinette, and threw them in prison. You can see where they and other nobles were held prisoner if you visit the Conciergerie. In January 1793, the king and queen were beheaded in front of a crowd at what is now the Place de la Concorde. Thousands of people were decapitated by the Guillotine during what was called The Reign of Terror. Besides the king and queen, the noble class and the defenders of it were put to death. The French celebrate Bastille Day, as we celebrate the Fourth of July.

A soldier named Napoleon united France and crowned himself "Master of France" in 1799. Napoleon continued the building frenzy that began during the Renaissance. The arches you see today along the rue de Rivoli were built by Napoleon, as was the Place de l'Etoile and the Church of the Madeline at Place Madeline. Napoleon also ordered the Arc de Triomphe to be built in 1806, in homage to his military triumphs. It was not finished, though until 1836, fifteen years after the dictator's death. Napoleon continued his conquering missions until he was forced in 1812 to withdraw from Moscow, and was then defeated in 1815 at Waterloo by the Prussians, Dutch and English. He was exiled to a British island named St. Helena and died in 1821. It is thought that he was poisoned.

After Napoleon's exile and death, a monarchy was reestablished until 1830 when it was again overthrown. Louis-Philippe was then elected king, and he ruled for the next eighteen years during a fairly peaceful and prosperous time. The oldest monument today in Paris, the Obelisk of Luxor, was brought to Paris in 1836. Paris's first railroad was opened, and France continued to prosper. Much of French cuisine was a product of this period.

In 1848, the poor working class began a series of revolts and forced Louis-Philippe out of office. Napoleon's nephew, Napoleon III, was then elected president of France. This period is known as the Second Republic. Napoleon took complete control by 1851 when he declared himself emperor. He is best known for forcibly redesigning Paris. Beginning in 1853, Napoleon commissioned Baron Haussmann to reorganize Paris into boulevards connected by a series of squares. He wanted to create the most elegant city in the world. Haussmann's reconstruction of Paris lasted seventeen years, and he is responsible for the way Paris looks today.

In 1870, Napoleon III was defeated by the Prussians in Sudan, where he was held prisoner with at least one hundred thousand of his soldiers. Germany then set up cannons outside of Paris and became a serious threat.

Trouble began brewing within Paris and set off another revolt, which resulted in the burning of the Tuileries castle (that is why you only see the gardens today), and another government overthrow. Marshall MacMahon was elected as president of France in 1873. This was the beginning of what is known as the Third Republic.

Paris flourished again. It became the site for four Universal Expositions (World's Fairs). During this period, from 1878 until 1937, many of Paris's monuments were built including the Eiffel Tower, the Grand and Petit Palais (which are art museums today), Trocadéro and Sacré-Coeur. In 1889, the Eiffel Tower was completed by an engineer, Gustave Eiffel, to celebrate the one hundredth anniversary of the French Revolution. Many Parisians considered it a controversial eyesore. It was supposed to be destroyed in 1909, but was saved when another engineer used the tower to hold an aerial for a new invention – the radio transmitter. The Paris Métro was also constructed during this time.

After World War I, an economic depression led to the formation of the Communist party. During the 1920s a lot of American writers came to Paris: F. Scott Fitzgerald, Gertrude Stein, and Ernest Hemingway all moved to Paris to write.

France declared war on Germany in 1939, after Germany invaded Poland. On June 12, 1940, Paris surrendered to the Germans during World War II. The Germans stayed in Paris for the next four years. During this time, France cooperated with the Nazis. When they finally left, France Resistance leader, General Charles de Gaulle marched with thousands of Parisians down the Champs-Elysées. He then became the president of France during its Fourth Republic.

In 1954, France went to war with its colony, Algeria, which wanted independence. In 1962, this war ended with Algeria being the winner.

In 1968, students revolted in Paris, as they did in the United States. But here, the effects were more devastating, nearly causing government collapse and war.

In 1981, Francois Mitterand was elected as the first socialist president of France since World War II. This caused quite a stir among France's wealthy citizens, many of whom invested their money outside of France.

Euro Disney opened in the Paris suburb Marné-la-Valee in 1992. It has since been renamed Disneyland Paris.

In the mid-1990s, Paris faced terrorist threats that included a bombing on the metro, killing seven passengers and injuring 150 people.

Just For Kids: Amusement Parks

Jardin D'Acclimation
Bois de Boulogne
750016 Paris
Tel: 01-40-67-90-82
Métro: Sablons
Admission: The park has an entry fee of 2.50 € and a *carnet* (book of fourteen tickets) costs 25 €. You have to pay with tickets for most of the rides and games.
Hours:
Winter: 10 a.m. to 6 p.m.
Summer: 10 a.m. to 7 p.m.

    The park is about a ten-minute walk from the métro station, so bring an umbrella stroller if you have a small child who won't want to walk, or will be too exhausted after all that fun, to walk back. There is also a miniature train that leaves from Porte Maillot from 1:30 p.m. to 6 p.m. Wednesdays, Saturdays, and Sundays and every day during school vacations.
    This is the best – a park just for kids in the top end of the Bois de Boulogne (near Neuilly, but still Paris). It is ideal for small children, but could certainly be fun up until about age twelve. Teenagers and ultrasophisticated eleven – and twelve-year-olds may think it's dumb. Food, cotton candy, balloons, sand pails, shovels, and balls are sold near

the front of the park. There are also restaurants and snack bars. You'll find an entire area of rides including two merry-go-rounds, an enchanted river ride where kids go down a small river in a boat, a Dumbo ride, an Aladdin and teacup ride, bumper cars (you have to be ten), a kids' car track (no steering needed), a roller coaster, a small train and more. A game area has shooting booths, fishing (plastic fish), ball throwing challenges, dart balloon booth, video arcade, and flash painting where you squirt in colors that revolve around to create an abstract painting.

There are also pony rides, where the children are led around on calm-looking ponies that are attached on a rope. Le Poney Club is also an equestrian center for real riders. Reservations can be made at: 01-45-01-97-97.

Two bears live in a large, rocky area and are easy for kids to see, because there are several huge Plexiglas windows that begin at the ground. Birds and monkeys are in floor-to-ceiling open or glassed habitats, so children may also easily view them. A small farm zoo has chickens, rabbits, donkeys, goats, pigs, cows, sheep, ducks, and geese. There is also a vegetable garden where raspberries, black currents, and leeks are grown. Beyond this, there is an "Exploradome," a small interactive science center for kids three and up.

Nearby is the Maison Enchantée for children one through twelve. It's open Wednesdays, Saturdays, Sundays and vacation days. To be on the safe side, reservations may be made at 01-40-67-92-87. It has Nintendo, little cars, computer games, a little, plastic slide, a Lego table, a brio table, and a slide that ends up in a bunch of balls, as well as a protected play area for tiny children. Everyone has to remove their shoes before they are allowed to enter.

Across from the Maison Enchantée, there is an amazing playground with huge sand lots and fantastic, new-age teeter-totters made of metal and topped by ladybugs, bees, butterflies, and grasshoppers, a fire engine for climbing, swings and a climbing area with tunnels.

For kids eight through twelve, there is a bike track with circuits (bikes, helmets and supervision provided). This is free and is supposed to be like the one that trains the police. Reservations: 01-45-01-20-92.

There is also a bowling alley with a video game arcade. Reservations: 01-53-64-93-14, and miniature golf reservations: 01-40-67-15-17.

Additionally, there is an enclosed trampoline, and one of those games children can get into and roll around in balls.

On Wednesday and Sunday, there is a circus at 3:00. On Saturday it is at 4:30. The show is an hour and a half. It also performs during vacations, so you can call and check the days and hours. A thirty-minute puppet show is offered free on Wednesdays and weekends at three and four o'clock. Reservations: 01-45-01-53-52.

If this is not enough, there is le Musée en Herbe, a children's museum. Here, you wander into rooms visualizing the evolution of art. The first features prehistoric cave art, then a storm like the ones the artist Turner painted, an explorer room, a seventeenth-century peasant room with a table and fireplace, and a Picasso room complete with a puzzle and mirror. There are also temporary exhibits. While I was visiting, there was an exhibit about discovering sculptures with all different colors of modeling clay to try. It was for children three to six years old. Before this, there was an interactive African exhibit for children four and up.

Parc Asterix
60128 Plailly
Adult: 32 €
Child (3-11): 23 €, under three is free
Telephone (.15 € per minute charge): 08-91-67-67-11
Open: April to October
9:30 a.m. to 7 p.m. – check time before leaving.

This theme park is thirty kilometers from Paris and has twenty-seven attractions, seven adventure areas and six shows. Most of the attractions center on the Asterix comic books. Asterix and Obelix (his friend) are two brave Gaulois (ancestors to the French) fighting the Roman army. The park features an eighteenth-century fight show between French *mousquetaires* (as in three), and the Tonnerre de Zeus, a rollercoaster that takes you high off the ground and over a Gaelic forest, a giant baby in a self-propelled baby carriage and a dolphinarium. You may also watch artisans blowing glass, and working with wood and stone in streets that are constructed to look like medieval Paris. The park is considerably less crowded during the week.

Getting there: RER B3 from Châtelet or Gare du Nord, direction Roissy. Get off at Charles-de-Gaulle 1 and take the shuttle bus, which leaves from the bus station at Roissy C/1 every half hour. Driving: take motorway A1 Paris-Lille to the Parc Asterix exit.

Disneyland
Marne-la-Vallée
Tel: 01-64-73-30-00
Tel. from U.S: 407-934-7639
Hours: The hours vary, so check ahead of time. Summer hours are generally 9 a.m. to anywhere between 8 and 11 p.m.
Admission: Adults (anyone over twelve): 40 €
Adults (anyone over twelve) Low Season (Jan. 6 to April 4): 29 €
Children: 30 €
Children (over three): 25 €

It's Disney. It's expensive, and it's packed in summer. It is also quite crowded, cold, and damp in April (school break) with lines more than forty-five minutes long. If your children know about it, they will want to go there. It's smaller than the Disney World in Orlando, so make a day of it, as the park is only about twenty miles outside of Paris. One hint: buy your tickets ahead of time in Paris at the Paris Tourist Office at 127 av. des Champs-Elysées, Galeries Lafayette department store in Paris, Airport Tourism offices (Charles De Gaulle and Orly), at the Disney Stores (44 av. des Champs-Elysées), Virgin Megastores and the FNAC chains. This way you won't have to wait in the long line. Disney also recommends that people arrive early and go to the popular rides immediately. These include Big Thunder Mountain, Indiana Jones, Dumbo, the Flying Elephant, Star Tours, Orbitron, Autopia, and most other rides in Fantasyland. Many of the lines for these rides become unbearable by the afternoon. Adventure Island and Alice's Curious Labyrinth generally do not have long lines. Pirates of the Caribbean and It's a Small World have a fast turnover.

You'll see the parades best if you watch them from their starting points. Unfortunately, you need to get a place at least a half an hour before an event. If you decide to skip the parades, go to the popular rides, because they tend to empty out for the parades.

Food: There's a Planet Hollywood and McDonald's at the entrance as you get off the train and before you enter the park. I thought the food inside the park was expensive and not very good. The fast food you buy walking around, like waffles, is better.

Driving Directions: Take the A4 Autoroute east towards Reims, Nancy, and Metz (this is also known as *autoroute de l'est*). The park is about thirty-two kilometers outside of Paris. Take exit 14 and follow the signs.

Train: This may sound complicated, but it's really easy. I highly recommend it. Pick up the RER train service from Paris from any station on the A4 line train (not the A2).

These stations include La Défense, Charles de Gaulle-Etoille, Auber, Châtelet les Halles, Gare de Lyon and Nation. Be sure that you are headed toward Marne-la-Vallée-Chessy, and that the illuminated signs actually say that the train stops here, as some trains end before this stop or fork off onto another route. Avoid trains that say destination "Boissy." The ride is forty minutes and easy. The Marne-la-Vallée/Chessy train station is between Disney Village and the park entrance, a couple minutes' walk from the main gate. Turn right after leaving the station to get to the park, or left for Disney Village and the hotel complex.

English language RER information is: 01-36-68-41-14

Parks and Playgrounds

Good news! You may remember the *Pelouse Interdite* law in Paris, which banned everyone from the grass. This law changed in April 1997, and there are only a few parks where people have to keep off the grass. These include Tuileries, Luxembourg, Monceau and Palais Royal. Most of the big parks have pay bathrooms, and children are usually free.

First Arrondissement

Tuileries
Place de la Concorde, rue de Rivoli, Avenue du Gal-Lemonnier, quai des Tuileries
Métro: Tuileries, Concorde

Let off some steam after the Louvre. Here, you'll find a merry-go-round, swings, sandboxes, pony and donkey rides, and from mid-June to late August and Christmas, a Ferris wheel. On the Louvre side there is a pond where children rent and sail boats in the summer for 1.5 €. The pony rides are 2.28 € per child, and the ponies and donkeys are all tied together and led. The merry-go-round is 1.5 €, and there is a cotton candy (*barbe au papa*) stand next to the ticket booth. During the summer, there is a fair here, with rides and games galore. It's not cheap. Most rides are between 1.5 € and 3 €, so bring plenty of cash.

Fifth Arrondissement

Jardin des Plantes
Place Valhubert, rue Buffon or rue Geoffroy-St-Hilaire
75005 Paris
Métro: Austerlitz or Jussieu
Tel: 01-40-79-30-00

Combine a visit to this seventy-four–acre botanical garden with your trip to the Natural History Museum. The gardens have beautiful roses, irises, and plants. Here, you'll also find a huge maze you can wander through and a playground (for those under ten) which has a fantastic dinosaur skeleton slide, sandbox, swings and climbing toys. There is also Paris's oldest zoo (*ménagerie*) with camels, bison, bears, antelopes, lions, monkeys, reptiles, and birds of prey. The zoo's rather bizarre history began right after the revolution when it was built to house the few animals left from the royal zoo at Versailles. It gradually added animals until the siege of Paris in 1870 and 1871, when the animals were eaten by the rich.

Sixth Arrondissement

Jardin du Luxembourg
Bd. Saint Michel, rue de Vaugirard, rue Guynemer
Métro: Saint-Sulpice

Although people are told to keep off the grass throughout most of this park, there is an area of this enormous lawn where kids can run and play. The Luxembourg has something for everyone, beautiful gardens for grown-ups and fantastic play areas for a wide range of ages. It also has pony rides, a merry-go-round (where the man holds up hoops, kids grab with a stick), and puppet shows at 4 p.m. daily with an extra 11 a.m. show on Saturday and Sunday. There is a special area with swings, sandboxes, and a wading pool for children under six, as well as basketball hoops for older kids. Don't miss the pay play area, open from 10 a.m. to 7 p.m. It's 2.29 € per child and 1.37 € for an adult, and is well worth it. Also in the gardens, visit the *orangerie* and the *rucher* which houses twenty million bees.

Square Boucicaut
Corner of rue de Seine and rue Babylone
Métro: Sèvres-Babylone

Conveniently located right across from the Bon Marché department store, this area is especially designed for small children. It has swings, slides, sandboxes, climbing and jumping toys and a merry-go-round with cars. Consider it payment for a few stolen moments of shopping. It's also perfect if you're staying at Lutetia.

Seventh Arrondissement

Champ-de-Mars
Entrance at l'Ecole Militaire and the Eiffel Tower
Métro: Ecole Militaire

After a visit to the Eiffel Tower, your children can take a pony ride, go on a merry-go-round, slide, climb, and generally run wild.

Eighth Arrondissement

Parc Monceau
78 rue de le Courcelles, 113 bd. Malesherbes, place Rio-de-Janeiro, place du Général-Brocard
Métro: Monceau

This pretty park has swings, slides, climbing structures, sandboxes and a merry-go-round, a playhouse and a train.

Jardin des Champs-Elysées
Av. des Champs-Elysées
Métro: Franklin Roosevelt, Champs-Elyseés-Clemenceau, Concorde

The famous garden where Proust found Albertine now has sandboxes, a minislide, a climbing structure and a merry-go-round on Wednesday and weekends.

Twelfth Arrondissement

Parc Floral
Route de Champ de Manoeuvre
750012 Paris
Tel: 01-49-57-24-84
Métro: Château de Vincennes
Transfer to the 112 bus to Parc Floral or walk – it's about fifteen minutes.

Hours:
Summer: 9:30 a.m. to 8 p.m. daily
Winter: 9:30 a.m. to 5 p.m. daily
Adults: 1.52 €
Children six to eighteen: .38 €

This enormous playground offers everything a kid could want. There are swings, pulleys, slides, climbing apparatus and a miniature train that costs .91 € per ride. Double and triple-seated bike carts are rented near the ticket booth. One person pedals and the rest of the family enjoys the park. The bikes can carry up to six or seven people, and cost 6.40 € and 9.15 € per half hour, depending on size. There are also motorcars on a track for .91 € per ride. A child has to be over ten to ride without an adult. The rides and bikes are available from March 13 through September 5. In the Serre de Papillons, you can walk among fifty species of butterflies that inhabit the Ile-de-France region. The butterfly greenhouse is open from May to October from 1:30 p.m. to 5:15 p.m. and weekends and holidays from 1:30 p.m. until 6:15 p.m. and is free. The Paris-Nature is a children's educational nature center which has games, books, and exhibitions (in French).

Promenade Plantée and Jardin de Reuilly
Corner of av. Ledru-Rollin and av. Daumesnil
750012 Paris
Métro: Ledru-Rollin

This park features a former railroad station and a suspended walkway. The promenade stretches from the Bastille to the Bois de Vincennes. The Jardin de Reuilly is an enormous lawn, perfect for picnics or throwing a ball around. There is also a small playground.

Fourteenth Arrondissement

Parc Montsouris
Bd. Jourdan, av. Reille, av. du Pt-René-Coty
Métro: Cité Université

This pretty park has the observatory that gives the weather forecasts for all of Paris. Besides this, there are puppet shows, slides, seesaw, swings, sandboxes, a climbing toy with a slide, a merry-go-round and a lake with swans and ducks, that you may feed if you bring bread.

Sixteenth Arrondissement

Jardin de Trocadéro
Entrance at le Palais Chaillot and l'avenue New York
Métro: Trocadéro

This park is great for a stop after le Musée de la Marine. It has a view of the Eiffel Tower along with swings, sandboxes and slides, watchtower, merry-go-round and more.

Bois de Bologne
Jardin D'Acclimation

Wonderful. See "Just For Kids."

Nineteenth Arrondissement

La Villette
30 av. Corentin Cariou or 211 av. J. Jaures
Métro: Porte La Villette

    This park is on the same grounds as the science center, and is the largest park in Paris. Here, there are different theme gardens designated by age, and exceptionally comfortable chairs for the adults. Play hide-and-seek in a hilly garden with walkways that sway over small streams. Ride the rolling slide, power a windmill by pedaling, jump on a trampoline or dig in the sand.

Parc des Buttes-Chaumont
Rue de Crimée, rue Manin, rue Botzaris
Métro: Buttes-Chaumont or Botzaris

    This splendid park not only has playgrounds, but a man-made cave and waterfall. It is an excellent park for a picnic. Afterward, your kids can feed leftover bread to the hungry ducks in the lake. Buttes-Chaumont also has several small restaurants where you can buy lunch or drinks and sit outside. The playground areas with slides, swings, seesaws, climbing structures and sandboxes are open every day. These playgrounds are geared to smaller children, six or under. The pay merry-go-round, donkey rides, rocking horses and swings are open on Wednesday afternoons and weekends. There is a puppet show every day in good weather at 4:30 p.m., and short boat rides (.75 € roundtrip or .38 € one-way) across the small lake.

Monuments

Choose your monuments and museums wisely; there will be a limit to how much your kids will want to see. And remember, most stop selling tickets half an hour before closing time.

Eiffel Tower (Tour Eiffel)
Champ-de-Mars
75007 Paris
Tel: 01-44-11-23-23
Métro: Ecole-Militaire, Trocadéro or Bir Hakeim (none of these are very close)
RER: Champ-de-Mars-Tour-Eiffel
This is actually the nearest stop to the tower.
Hours from January 1 to June 13: 9:30 a.m. to 11 p.m.
June 14 to August 31: 9 a.m. to midnight
September 1 to December 31: 9:30 a.m. to 11 p.m.
The stairs, in the fall and winter, close at 6 p.m. They are open until midnight in the summer. Stair admission is 3 € for everyone.
Admission to Third Landing:
Adults: 10.20 €
Children under eighteen: 5.50 €
Second Floor: 7 € and 3.90 €
First Floor: 3.70 € and 2.30 €

Built as a temporary exhibit for the World's Fair in 1889, the Eiffel Tower is on the top of every kid's list. Don't visit too early, as it seems most crowded in the morning. Try to come on a clear day and go to the third stage, which has a nearly forty-mile view. If you have older children, the view at night is spectacular.

None of the métro stops are close, and the walk from Trocadéro is the nicest. If you are near an RER stop, you'll end up right near the Eiffel Tower if you get off at Champ-de-Mars.

Arc de Truimph
Place Charles-de-Gaulle-Etoile
75008 Paris
Tel: 01-55-37-73-77
Métro: Charles-de-Gaulle-Etoile
October 1 to March 31: 10 a.m. to 10:30 p.m.
April 1 to September 30: 9:30 a.m. to 11 p.m.
Adults: 7 €
Children over eleven: 4.5 €

To be honest, my children were more fascinated by the traffic here than the arch. It is the busiest hub in Paris, but there is an underground walkway to the arch that can be reached from the north side of the Champs-Elysées. It's possible to take an elevator or stairs to the top where there is an exhibition about the arch's history, which began when Napoleon commissioned it in 1806 to mark his victories. It was not completed, however, until 1836, fifteen years after Napoleon's death and during the reign of Louis-Philippe. In 1841, Napoleon's remains were exhumed from his grave and passed under the arch on the way to his tomb at Les Invalides. Since then, it's been an important part of France's state funerals. The Tomb of the Unknown Soldier, with its eternal flame, is also here, as is a small museum of the arch's history. The view from the observation deck is amazing, but if you're pressed for time or patience, and you've been to the top of the Eiffel Tower – skip it.

Place de la Concorde
Métro: Concord

Here's more traffic, but a lot of history. During the Reign of Terror, this was the home of the guillotine which beheaded the likes of Louis

XVI, Marie Antoinette, and Robespierre. The Place de la Concorde was built in 1757 in honor of King Louis XV. The statue of the king was torn down during the French Revolution in 1792. This is also the spot of the oldest man-made monument in Paris – an Egyptian obelisk from Luxor. It was created around 1200 BC and placed in Paris in 1836 after the viceroy of Egypt gave it as a gift to Louis Philippe.

Hôtel des Invalides
Place des Invalides
75007 Paris
Tel: 01-44-42-37-72
Métro: Varenne, Invalides, or Latour-Maubourg
June 15 to September 15: 10 a.m. to 6:45 p.m.
April to September 30: 10 a.m. to 5:45 p.m.
October to March 31: 10 a.m. to 4:45 p.m.
Admission: One ticket covers everything – Napoleon's tomb, the military museum and a museum of models of French monuments and towns
Adults: 7 €
Children twelve to eighteen: 5 €
Children under eleven: Free

This is the big gilded dome you've been wondering about. The main draw here is Napoleon's tomb, which is seven coffins, one inside the other. It's actually not that interesting, but the military museum is fun. Here you can see Napoleon's death mask his tent and tent bed, as well as a display of the bedroom he inhabited during his exile on the island of St. Helena at the time of his death. There are some strange things, including a stuffed dog that belonged to Napoleon, his hat, saddle, and sword. The rest of the museum displays the evolution of weapons and war throughout history, with everything from Viking swords to suits of armor. It has a certain fascination. Some of the antique swords and pistols are quite beautiful. The Musée des Plans-Reliefs may not impress children as it displays scale models of French towns and monuments. The building got its name because King Louis IV originally commissioned it in 1671 to house soldiers who were injured in his wars. The king had been dead a long time by the time it was finished.

Conciergerie
1 quai de l'Horloge
75001 Paris
Tel: 01-53-73-78-50
Métro: Cité, Châtelet or Les Halles
Hours: 9:30 a.m. to 6 p.m.
Admission:
Adults: 7 €
Children: Free
You may buy a ticket that includes Saint Chapelle which is nearby.

More blood! While this building is from the fourteenth century, it's most famous as the prison, and torture chamber, used for the nobility who were waiting to be guillotined, including Marie Antoinette. You can see her furnished prison cell, as well as a few others. There were different classes of cells for rich and poor.

Arche de la Défense
Parvis de la Défense
Tel: 01-49-07-27-57
Métro: Grande Arche de la Défense
Hours: April 1 to September 30: 10 a.m. to 8 p.m.
October 1 to March 31: 10 a.m. to 7 p.m.
Adults: 7.50 €
Children six to seventeen: 6 €
Family Passes:
Two adults and one child: 15.5 €
Two adults and two children: 18.5 €
Two adults and three children: 21.5 €

This enormous, white, cubic building, located a few kilometers west of Paris, was built in 1989 for the two hundredth anniversary of the French Revolution by Danish architect, Otto van Speckelsen. It's basically an office building, so come here only if you're into views. Glass elevators take you to the roof, and it's a spectacular sight.

Versailles
Place d'Armes
Versailles
Tel: 01-30-83-77-88
Hours: May to September: 9 a.m. to 6:30 p.m.
October to May: 9 a.m. to 5:30 p.m.
Closed on Mondays
Admission: 7.50 € for adults
Children under eighteen: Free

Getting there: Take the RER C train to the Versailles-Rive-Gauche station from Musée D'Orsay, St-Michel, Gare d'Austerlitz, Pont d'Alma, Champ-de-Mars, Invalides or Javel stations. The train leaves about every fifteen minutes and the ride is half an hour.

The gardens and fountains at Versailles are beautiful, so if possible, go in good weather. My children were mainly impressed by the fact that kings and queens had lived there and that some had been beheaded. The great halls and gilded furniture were not the draw, but the whole picture got them talking about the French Revolution. The gardens are open every good-weather day in summer from 7 a.m. to sunset, and in winter from 8 a.m. until sunset. Admission is 3 €.

Religious Monuments

Nôtre Dame
Place du Parvis-Nôtre Dame
75004 Paris
Tel: 01-42-34-56-10
Métro: Cité and St-Michel
Hours: 8 a.m. to 7 p.m.
Admission to the church: free
Admission to the towers:
Adults: 5.34 €
Children twelve to twenty-five: 3.50 €
Free for under twelve and over sixty
Crypt admission: 5 €

Nôtre Dame is truly the essence of Paris, so try and see it. With Disney's *Hunchback of Notre Dame*, this splendid church holds a new allure for children. Although, quite honestly, once they get there, it's just a big (boring) church to them. One cool item is the brass plaque in front of the main doorway, marking the point from which all distances in France are calculated from Paris. The cathedral is still very much used, with six masses on Sunday and four on every other day. It took nearly two hundred years to build Nôtre Dame, and the cathedral was completed in 1330. During the French Revolution, much of Nôtre Dame was plundered and destroyed as the church was linked to the noble class. In the mid-1800s the architect Viollet-le-Duc restored it. Today the cathedral is still being renovated, and outside it is encased in scaffolding. While you will be impressed by the church's grace and beauty, your children will mainly be interested in climbing to the top. The towers are generally open from April through September: 9:30 a.m. to 7:30 p.m., and October through March: 10 a.m. to 5 p.m. They are closed on Sunday.

The initial climb of the North Tower is nearly four hundred steps. You then cross over to the south tower, which is full of carved gargoyles and other monsters. Here, you may also (with a guide) visit the famous bell tower. The south tower may then be climbed up further to the top. When you descend, you will pass a room devoted to Nôtre Dame's history.

With kids in tow, you will probably want to skip the treasury, but do try to go to the crypt. This is an archeological site that was discovered in front of the cathedral. Here are the remains of former churches built on this site, as well as relics left from them. You can walk down into a chamber with the cellars of medieval houses and third-century Gallo-Roman ramparts.

Sacré-Coeur
Place du Parvis du Sacré-Coeur
75018 Paris
Tel: 01-53-41-89-00
Métro: Anvers, Abbesses, Chateau-Rouge, Lamarck-Caulaincourt
Hours: 9 a.m. to 5:45 p.m.

On Montmartre's hill, the Sacré-Coeur is huge and white and contains beautiful mosaics. You can take a funicular part or all the way up. All you need is a métro ticket. While Sacré-Coeur looks Byzantine and very old, it was actually built as a reaction to the despair caused by France's defeat in the Franco-Prussian War in 1870. It was completed in 1914 but not consecrated until 1919 because of World War I. You can climb up to the dome, which has a great view of Paris. There is a lot of touristy junk and restaurants surrounding the church. But if you walk down, you'll see the only vineyard left in Paris.

Mémorial du Martyr Juif Inconnu (Memorial to the Unknown Jewish Martyr)
37 rue de Turenne
75004 Paris
Tel: 01-42-77-44-72
Métro: Saint-Paul or Pont Marie
Hours: Monday through Friday – 10 a.m. to 1 p.m. and 2 p.m. to 5:30 p.m.
Closed on Saturdays and Jewish holidays
Adults: 2.30 €

A memorial dedicated to the six million Jews who died during World War II. Built in 1956, it's been expanded over the years and contains documents and photos of Nazi camps. There are also temporary exhibitions.

Sainte Chapelle
4 bd. du Palais
75001 Paris
Tel: 01-53-73-78-51
Métro: Cité
Hours: Open every day from 9:30 a.m. to 6 p.m.
Adults: 5.50 €
Children over seventeen: 3.50 €
Good idea: You may buy a combo ticket to see Saint Chapelle and the Conciergerie

This is the most beautiful place in Paris. Even if your children are young, try to stop here (on a sunny day). Step in, and you'll be surrounded by fifteen breathtaking windows. It's like being inside jewels. The ceiling is magically sprinkled with stars. Saint Chapelle was built in 1248 by Louis IX, as a place to showcase what he thought was Christ's Crown of Thorns and other religious relics.

Museums

All national museums are free the first Sunday of every month. Avoid visiting on this day.

La Cité des Sciences et de L'Industrie
30 av. Corentin-Cariou
75019 Paris
Tel: 01-40-05-80-00 and 01-40-05-70-00
Métro: Porte de la Villette
Hours: 10 a.m. to 6 p.m., Sunday 10 a.m. to 7 p.m.
Closed on Mondays
Adults Main Exhibit: 7.50 €
Children seven to seventeen: 5.50 €
Children under seven: Free
Planetarium admission: 3 €
Géode admission: 8.75 € for adults and 6.75 € for children
Cité des Enfants admission: 5 €
Cinéxe: Adults are 5.20 € and children are 4.50 €

    Reservations and additional tickets are required for some exhibits (Cité des Enfants and Techno City), which have three to four sessions daily with more on Wednesdays and weekends.
    This enormous science museum appeals to all different ages, and you can easily spend the day here. My one caution is that everything is in French, which can make it difficult if you have kids who like detail. If not, I think it's fun. There is a main exhibit, an interactive area (Cité des Enfants), Techno City, an aquarium, a planetarium, the Géode, which

offers omnimax movies on a 180-degree curved screen every hour to children over three, and the Cinéxe – a realistic flight simulation for children over six (no pregnant women).

The museum can be a bit overwhelming, so take some time to decide what you want to do before you get there. The permanent exhibitions are organized into three main sections, each offering between two hundred and three hundred presentations. A sampling: space and ocean, energy and the environment, aeronautics, mathematics, computer science, rocks and volcanoes, and stars and galaxies. Explanations are in French, but English headsets and a guide in English are available. I strongly recommend one or the other.

Your ticket to the main exhibit entitles you to visit the planetarium. You can reserve a seat for the planetarium by collecting a ticket from the visitor's forum, which also has a daily program of shows.

Visitors are allowed to go in and out of the museum four times within a day with one ticket. This means you can take a picnic break in the adjacent park, visit the submarine, the Argonaut, a real 1950s submarine which was disarmed in 1982 – or see a movie in the Géode (English headsets are available). Your ticket also allows you into the aquarium, which has more than two hundred species of fish, mollusks, crustaceans and plants from Mediterranean coastal waters.

Cité des Enfants is a separate section with interactive activities that requires a separate admission ticket. Here, three-to-five-year-olds can play all kinds of educational games. Five-to-twelve-year-olds have their own area in which they experiment with pumps, gear and robots, learn about and see inside of the human body and explore communicating techniques. Each session lasts an hour and a half, and the schedule is available at the reception desk. Parents must stay with their children, and the two, age-based facilities are completely independent. Call 01-40-05-12-12 for reservations, or fax 01-40-05-81-90.

Techno City is an exhibit for children over eleven, requiring a reservation and a separate ticket. It has five permanent themes: mechanisms in motion, manufacturing techniques, sensors and automatic devices, development of a prototype, and designing a computer program. Techno City is open to the public Wednesdays, Saturdays and school holidays. The rest of the week, the schools use it. Each session is an hour and a half.

Cité de la Musique
221 av. Jean-Jaures
75019 Paris
Tel: 01-44-84-44-84
Métro: Porte de Pantin
Hours: Tuesday through Saturday: from 12 noon to 6 p.m., Sunday: 10 a.m. to 6 p.m.
Closed on Monday and Bank Holidays
Adults: 6.10 €
Children: 4.80 €

A museum of music in which more than four thousand instruments are displayed ranging from the Middle Ages to modern. See everything from a zither to an electric guitar. Audio phones are included with admission, and music plays as you walk from instrument to instrument. This museum would definitely appeal to classical music lovers, but would probably bore small children. The museum also houses concert halls, a music school and a music library. There is a nice café (run by the Costes brothers) for lunch or a snack.

Musée National des Arts d'Afrique et d'Océanique
293 av. Daumesnil
75012 Paris
Tel: 01-44-74-84-80
Métro: Porte Dorée
Hours: 10 a.m. to 5:30 p.m.
Closed on Tuesdays
Adults: 5.30 €
Children under eighteen: Free

Here is Paris's aquarium, complete with two pits holding real crocodiles and turtles. Big hit. This museum also displays collection of African and oceanic art. This section will probably not interest your kids, so head down the stairs to the fish. Right near the Bois des Vincennes, which also has a great park and zoo.

Musée de la Marine
Palais de Chaillot
Place du Trocadéro
75016 Paris
Tel: 01-53-65-69-69
Métro: Trocadéro
Hours: 10 a.m. to 5:30 p.m.
Closed on Tuesdays
Adults: 5.75 €
Children eight to twenty-five and seniors: 3.85 €

This museum appeals to boat enthusiasts. Here you'll see lots of models of old ships, including a barge made for Napoleon I, exhibits explaining ancient shipbuilding, fishing and sea lore. The elaborate collection documents ships from the seventeenth century to today. There are also many ocean-related artifacts, art, and documents.

Musée National d'Histoire Naturelle (Museum of Natural History)
57 rue Cuvier
75005 Paris
Tel: 01-40-79-30-00
Métro: Gare d'Austerlitz or Jussieu
Gallery of Evolution: 10 a.m. to 6 p.m. weekdays (closed on Tuesdays) and 10 a.m. to 10 p.m. Friday through Sunday
Other galleries: 10 a.m. to 5 p.m.
Closed on Tuesdays
Admission: Varies depending upon the galleries. For the Gallery of Evolution, it's 7 € for adults and 5 € for children over five. The other galleries are 5 € and 3 €. There is a free coatcheck, which is handy on a wet day.

This popular museum in the Jardin des Plantes (park), offers nature and science exhibits, including an eighty-five-foot whale skeleton at its entrance. The Grand Gallery of Evolution is the main draw here – and your kids will love it. There are explanations in all different languages, including English, in pull-out wooden boxes near each exhibit. There is a cool electronic display of the births and deaths in the world population. You watch it constantly change. Don't miss the Noah's Ark of stuffed real animals – which is in the center of the main floor – and be sure and visit the area which uses movie effects to recreate the atmosphere of the Savannah. My kids loved an evolution exhibit that had cards for imprinting. They had to find the different sources. The other galleries cover paleobotany (plant fossils), mineralogy, entomology and anatomy. Afterwards, there is an enormous dinosaur skeleton slide in the Jardin des Plants as well as a small zoo.

Musée Grévin: Wax Museum
10 bd. Montmartre
75009 Paris
Tel: 01-47-70-85-05
Métro: Grands Boulevards
Hours: Open Monday through Friday 10 a.m. to 6:30 p.m., Saturday and Sunday 10 a.m. to 7 p.m.
Adults: 16 €
Children six to fourteen: 9 €

A French history lesson in wax that's both educational and entertaining. There are over 450 wax figures in the first privately owned French museum created by journalist Arthur Meyer in 1882. The French revolution comes alive with scenes including Louis XVI and Marie Antoinette in prison. There are also modern wax heroes including Madonna, Michael Jackson, and Marilyn Monroe. Sound and light shows are performed here regularly, but it gets pitch dark which may be scary for small children. I know I didn't like it.

Musée Carnavalet
23 rue de Sévigné
75003 Paris
Tel: 01-44-59-58-58
Métro: Saint-Paul
Hours: 10 a.m. to 6 p.m.

Closed on Mondays
Admission: Adults are 6 €, children are free

If your kids are ten or older, and interested in history, this museum is terrific. Its collections visually show Paris's history through unusual historical artifacts. On the ground floor there are antique Parisian shop signs and scale models of the city. Most of the museum is organized into period rooms giving the feel of how people lived. Marcel Proust's cork-lined bedroom is showcased here (open from 10:30 a.m. to 12:30 p.m.) along with many items from the French Revolution. The museum itself is beautiful. It's in a Renaissance mansion that once belonged to Madame de Sévigné. Madame was the author of a famous collection of letters that describe the court of Louis XIV. There are several rooms dedicated to her lifestyle. The museum is big, and you'll probably want to skip around. Small children will think it looks like a bunch of old furniture and paintings.

Musée de la Curiosité
Espace Magique de Marais
11 rue Saint-Paul
75004 Paris
Tel: 01-42-72-13-26
Métro: Saint-Paul
Hours: Wednesday, Saturday and Sunday from 2 to 7 p.m.
Adults: 7 €
Children three to twelve: 5 €

A magic museum. Here, kids can see optical illusions, psychic phenomena and magic props, including some belonging to Houdini. There's a magic show every half hour. The friendly magician shows children how some of the tricks are done and has kids from the audience help him. It's easy to understand even if you don't speak French.

Palais de la Découverte
Av. Franklin D Roosevelt
75008 Paris

Tel: 01-56-43-20-20 for recorded information
Other information: 01-56-43-20-21
Métro: Franklin D. Roosevelt
Hours: Tuesday through Saturday from 9:30 a.m. to 6 p.m.
Sunday: 10 a.m. to 7 p.m.
Closed on Mondays
Adults: 6.50 €
Children seven and up: 4 €
Under five: free
Planetarium: 3.10 €

A science museum in which kids can learn about centrifugal force and see an ant colony. There is an interactive area and a planetarium for which you need reservations ahead of time. The planetarium shows are at 11 a.m., 2 p.m., 3:15 p.m., and 4:30 p.m. On weekends, a 5:30-p.m. show is added. This museum is easily accessible and a much smaller science museum than La Villette. It's a good half-day choice that features computerized memory games, exhibits on learning and a large section on electricity. Explanations are in French, but because it's interactive, anyone can have fun.

Musée de la Poupée
Impasse Berthaud at the beginning of 22 rue Rambuteau
75003 Paris
Tel: 01-42-72-73-11
Métro: Rambuteau
Hours: Tuesday through Sunday from 10 a.m. to 6 p.m.
Thursday the museum has late hours from 8 p.m. to 10:30 p.m.
Closed on Mondays and Holidays
Adults: 6 €
Children: 3 €

This museum has a collection of thirty dolls spanning 1860 to 1960. Most are porcelain and all are behind glass. Unless you have a total doll freak, it's not worth visiting. Special temporary doll and toy exhibits are also held here.

Musée d'art et d'histoire du Judaïsme
71 rue du Temple
75003 Paris
Tel: 01-53-01-86-60
Métro: Rambuteau, Hôtel de Ville
Hours: Monday through Friday from 11 a.m. to 6 p.m., Sunday 10 a.m. to 6 p.m.
Closed on Saturdays
Adults: 6.10 €
Children under eighteen: Free

This new museum is in a seventeenth-century mansion in the Marais district. It features both the historic and the artistic aspects of European and North African Jewish culture in its thirteen rooms. There are works by Jewish masters like Chagall, Modigliani and Soutine and a collection of historical documents and artifacts. The timeframe spans the Middle Ages to the present, and would probably only be interesting to an older child with a strong interest in Judaism. It would be perfect for a child who was studying to have a bar or bat mitzvah. There is a moving art installation by the artist Christian Boltanski with the names and the deportation dates of the former inhabitants of the building in which the museum is housed.

Art Museums

One of the great things about Paris is the number of small museums. These are quick and manageable – a perfect child dose. The Louvre is easy, if you stick to just seeing a few things.

Louvre
34 quai du Louvre
75001 Paris
Tel: 01-40-20-50-50
Métro: Palais-Royale or Musée de Louvre
Hours: Thursday, Friday and Saturday from 9 a.m. to 6 p.m., Monday and Wednesday 10 a.m. to 9:45 p.m.

Closed on Tuesdays
Adults: 13 € (ticket that includes everything in the museum)
Children under eighteen: Free
Sunday admission is 9.50 €, as is admission after 3 p.m.

This is the biggest museum in the world, so choose what you want to see ahead of time. Most kids want to visit the *Mona Lisa* and the *Venus de Milo*. The crowd in front of the Mona Lisa is a scene, with tourists pushing and shoving, so go early. There is also an Egyptian mummy section and a wonderful new sculpture wing. My kids wanted to know where all the art came from. Much of it belonged to the kings of France, collections have been donated, and some has been purchased by the state.

Quick Bite: For lunch or a snack, the Carrousel du Louvre, which is a shopping center underneath the Louvre, has a food court – hamburgers, tapas, salads, desserts, and muffins.

Musée d'Orsay
62 rue de Lille
75007 Paris
Tel: 01-40-49-48-14
Métro: Solférino
Hours: Tuesday, Wednesday, Friday, and Saturday from 10 a.m. to 6 p.m. (in summer the museum usually opens at 9 a.m.); Thursday 10 a.m. to 9:45 p.m.; Sunday 9 a.m. to 6 p.m.
Closed on Mondays
Adults: 7 € (additional fee for special exhibits)
Children under eighteen: Free

The building alone leaves a lasting impression. The Musée d'Orsay is in a restored railroad station that has an arched-glassed roof with an enormous, beautiful clock. The collections of paintings, sculpture, architecture and photographs are from 1848 to 1914. This spans the historical period between the beginning of France's Second Empire and World War I. The museum is home to many of France's Impressionist paintings as well as Post-Impressionists, who are displayed on the top floor. Check out Manet's famous *Picnic on the Grass*, Monet's *Poppy Field* and Whistler's *Mother*.

Musée Picasso
5 rue de Thorigny
75003 Paris
Tel: 01-42-71-25-21
Métro: Saint-Paul, Filles du Calvaire or Chemin-Vert
Hours: April through September open from 9:30 a.m. to 6 p.m., October through March open from 9:30 a.m. to 5:30 p.m.
Closed on Tuesdays
Adults: 5.50 €
Children under eighteen: Free

This is an excellent small museum, which can be easily seen in less than an hour. It has the largest collection of Picassos in the world as well as paintings by other artists that Picasso collected. Picasso's family donated these paintings, sculptures, sketches, collages and ceramics as a $50-million break on inheritance taxes. Afterwards, you can visit the adjacent Jewish quarter. Go down rue de Rosiers.

Musée Rodin
77 rue de Varenne
75007 Paris
Tel: 01-44-18-61-10
Métro: Varenne or Invalides
Hours: October to March from 9:30 a.m. to 4:45 p.m., April to September from 9:30 a.m. to 5:45 p.m.
Closed on Mondays
Adults: 5 €
Children under eighteen: Free

This small museum displays the sculpture of Auguste Rodin, and is easy for children to get through quickly. You also have the option of just visiting the gardens, which contain many of Rodin's well-known sculptures including *The Thinker* and *The Burghers of Calais*.

Centre Pompidou (Beaubourg)
Musée national d'art Moderne
Place Georges Pompidou
75004 Paris
Tel: 01-44-78-12-33
Métro: Rambuteau, Les Halles, Châtelet, or Hôtel-de-Ville
Hours: 11 a.m. to 9 p.m.
Closed on Tuesdays
Adults: 7 € (additional ticket needed for special exhibits for adults and children over thirteen)
Children under eighteen: Free

This museum of modern art reopened December 31, 1999, after an extensive renovation. The building itself is fun with its glass walls and colorful pipes, and the collection is happy and bright. The main escalator is in a glass tube which runs up the front of the building. Big fun! Its collection begins with Fauvism in 1905 and continues through today, featuring Matisse, Miro, Picasso, Kandinsky and twentieth-century architecture and design. This museum also houses Brancusi's workshop, which was willed to France and reconstructed here. The Stravinsky Fountain outside the museum has wonderful Nicki de St. Phalle and Jean Tinguely sculptures of lips, skeletons, snakes and more spouting water.

Musée Marmottan
2 rue Louis-Boilly
750016 Paris
Tel: 01-44-96-50-33
Métro: La Muette
Hours: 10 a.m. to 6 p.m.
Closed on Mondays
Adults: 6.50 €
Children eight to twenty-four: 4 €
Children under eight: Free

This collection belonged to the nineteenth-century industrialist Jules Marmottan and his son, Paul. Upon Paul's death, the collection and the house were left to the Académie des Beaux Arts. It is the second largest collection of Impressionists after the Musée D'Orsey. If you love Monet's *Water Lilies*, you will find some here. The museum also houses a collection of medieval miniatures and art and furniture from the Napoleonic period. This is a wonderful, accessible museum housed in a nineteenth-century mansion on the edge of the Bois de Boulogne.

Musée national de L'Orangerie des Tuilleries
Place de la Concorde
Jardin des Tuileries
75001 Paris
Tel: 01-42-97-48-16
Métro: Concorde
Hours: 9:45 a.m. to 5:15 p.m.
Closed on Tuesdays
Adults: 4.60 €
Children under eighteen: Free

A terrific little museum across from the Jeu de Paume with paintings from the end of the Impressionist era to 1930. Here, you'll find eight of Monet's *Water Lilies*, as well as works by Matisse, Renoir, Cézanne and Picasso. The water lilies were installed by Monet and wrap completely around two rooms. The museum is closed for renovations until 2005.

Galerie nationale de Jeu de Paumes
Place de la Concorde
Jardin des Tuileries
75001 Paris
Tel: 01-47-03-12-52
Métro: Concorde
Hours: Tuesday from 12 noon to 9:30 p.m.
Wednesday through Friday from 12 noon to 7 p.m.
Weekends: 10 a.m. to 7 p.m.

Closed on Mondays
Adults: 8 €
Children over thirteen: 6.50 €

This is the national exhibition gallery of contemporary art. The installations are temporary, so check to see what's current.

Petite Palais Musée
Av. Winston Churchill
75008 Paris
Tel: 01-42-65-12-73
Métro: Champs-Elysées-Clemenceau
Hours: 10 a.m. to 5:40 p.m.
Closed on Mondays
Adults: 7 €
Children: 3.50 €

Most people come here to see temporary exhibits, and there are some great ones. The museum's permanent collection belongs to the city of Paris and is erratic. Unless you have loads of time or a babysitter, I'd only come here to view a special exhibit.

- **Museum passes:** One-three-and five-day museum passes may be purchased at major métro stations, tourist offices, participating museums and monuments, and FNAC stores. The main advantage to these is that you don't have to stand in long ticket lines, and the visits are unlimited. These are really for adults, as most of the art museums have free entrance for children. You would still have to stand in line for museums that charged for children, like the Science Center, as well as at temporary exhibits, which are not covered by the pass. A one-day pass is 25 €, a three-day (consecutive) is 44 € and a five-day (consecutive) is 62 €.

List of Museums and Monuments Covered by the Pass:

Musée des Antiquités national de Saint-Germain-en-Laye
Arc de Triomphe
Musée de L'Armée
Musée d'Art et d'Histoire du Judaïsme
Musée national d'Art Moderne – Centre Georges Pompidou
Musée national des Arts d'Afrique et D'Océanie
Musée national des Arts Asiatiques – Guimet
Musée des Arts Décoratifs
Musée des Arts et Métiers
Musée national des Arts et Traditions Populaires
Musée d'Art Moderne de Ville de Paris
Musée de L'Assistance Publique – Hôpitaux de Paris
Maison de Balzac
Musée Bourdelle
Musée Carnavalet
Musée Cemuschi
Musée national de Céramique de Sevrés
Abbaye royale de Chaalis – Muse Jacqumart-Andre
Château de Champs-sur-Marne
Musée de Cinéma – Henri Langlois
Cité des Sciences et de l'Industrie – La Villette
Musée Cognacq-Jay
Musée national du Château de Compiegne
Conciergerie
Musée Condé – Château de Chantilly
Musée national de la Coopération Franco-Américaine – Chareau de Bierancourt
Musée national Eugène Delacroix
Musée department Maurice Denis – Le Prieure
Musée des Egouts de Paris
Musée D'Ennery
Musée national du Château de Fontainebleau
Musée national des Granges de Port-Royal

Musée Herbert
Muse Jean-Jaques Henner
Musée de L'Institut du Monde Arabe
Musée de la Légion d'Honneur et des Ordres de Chevalerie
Musée de Louvre
Château de Maisons-Laffitte
Musée national des châteaux de Malmaison et Bois-Preau
Musée de la Marine
Mémorial du Maréchal Leclerc de Hauteclocque de la Libération de Paris – Musée Jean Moulin
Musée de la Mode et du Textile
Musée de la Monnaie
Musée national des Monuments Francais
Musée Gustave Moreau
Château de Motte Tilly
Musée national de Moyen Age – Thermes de Cluny
Musée de la Musique – La Villette
Musée Nissim de Camondo
Tours de Nôtre-Dame
Crypte de Nôtre-Dame
Musée national de l'Orangerie des Tuileries
Musée de l'Ordre de la Libération
Musée d'Orsay
Panthéon
Musée du Petit Palais
Musée national Picasso Château de Pierrefonds
Musée des Plans-reliefs
Musée de la Poste
Château de Rambouillet
Musée national de la Renaissance – Château d'Ecouen
Musée Rodin
Maison d'Auguste Rodin a Meudon
Sainte-Chapelle
Basilique Saint-Denis
Musée National des Châteaux de Versailles et de Trianon

Maison de Victor Hugo
Musée de la Vie Romantique
Château de Vincennes
Musée Zadkine

Zoos

Château et Parc Zoologique de Thoiry
Château de Thoiry
78770 Thoiry en Yvelines
Tel: 01-34-87-53-76
Hours: Most days it opens at 10 a.m., but you should check.
Adults (to animal park): 20 €
Children three to twelve: 14 €
Château visits:
Adult: 4.30 €
Children: 3.50 €

    Zebras in your car, bears in the trees and antelopes in the road. An African safari park (and a castle!) with eighty species of animals (elephants, camels, lions, tigers, giraffes, zebras, and ostriches) that wander the sprawling grounds. We even saw several piles of ostrich eggs. There is a small train that goes through the gardens, so little ones can glimpse some of the nonferocious animals. Otherwise you need a car for animal viewing, as well as getting to Thoiry. If you open your car windows in the nonferocious areas, be prepared for animals coming up and into the car to view you (and to see if there's any good food). There is also a reptile house and a self-service lunch place with a children's meal of a hamburger (no bun), fries, and a juice box. There are also dishes like chicken, quiche, and salads.

Driving Directions: From Paris take motorway A13, then the A12/N12 motorway direction to Dreux. At Pontrachain take the D11 towards Thoiry. It is about thirty minutes outside of Paris.

Train: SCNF train from Paris-Montparnasse station to Montfort l'Amaury and then a taxi to Thoiry.

La Ferme de Paris
Route du Pesage
Bois des Vincennes
Tel: 01-43-28-47-63
Métro: Château de Vincennes
Adults: 3.50 €
Children: 1.25 €

This is a real twelve-acre farm in Paris! Here, Parisian schoolchildren learn about life on the farm, tending to and feeding the animals, and participating in the growth and use of farm products like grain and milk. The vegetable garden is also for the children, who sow, tend, and harvest vegetables that are then prepared in the farm's kitchen. Because schools use it during the week, the farm is only open on weekends (during school) from April through October (1:30 to 7 p.m.) and November through March (1:30 to 5 p.m.). It's open daily in the summer, and milking is at 4 p.m. every day. The children watch as a man cleans the cow's udders, sprays the kids with milk, and then directs the stream into a bucket. Eventually, he hooks the cow to a milking machine, and the milk travels through a tube in the ceiling to a holding tank. This is the place where I had my major Parisian mishap. An affectionate, large calf reached her head through the metal fence, grabbed my dress, and refused to let go. Eventually, she relented and I escaped with a few teeth marks and cow drool on my dress.

Ménagerie du Jardin des Plantes
57 rue Cuvier
75005 Paris
Métro: Jussieu, Gare d'Austerlitz
Tel: 01-40-79-37-94
Adults: 6 €
Children under sixteen: 3.50 €

Visit here after you're done with the natural history museum. You'll find camels, antelopes, leopards, reptiles, flamingos, and more. This is the oldest zoo in Paris, built right after the revolution to house the few animals left from the royal zoo at Versailles. Animals were added, but then eaten by the rich during the siege of 1871.

Oddball Activities

Sewers *(Égouts)*
Pont d'Alma, facing 93 quai d'Orsay
75007 Paris
Tel: 01-53-68-27-81
Métro: Alma Marceau
Hours: From May to October, the sewers are open Saturday through Wednesday from 11 a.m. to 5 p.m.
The rest of the year (except closed three weeks in January), Wednesday through Saturday from 11 a.m. to 4 p.m.
Adults: 3.80 €
Children five to twelve: 3.05 €

The visit to Paris's 1300 miles of sewers consists of a movie on the history of Paris sewers, a small museum, and a foray into *les égouts*. How do I say this politely? It stinks, and is actually not terribly exciting. Tours are given in English, as well as French, so you may want to wait for English to be sure you understand the history and mechanics. Be aware that there is often a wait – and that the sewers will close in bad weather. Wear durable shoes, as the ground is wet.

France Miniature
25 route de Masnil
78990 Elancourt
Tel: 01-30-16-16-30
Hours: France Miniature is usually open from April to November from 10 a.m. to 7 p.m.

To be sure, call or check website: www.franceminiature.com
Adults: 13 €
Children four to fourteen: 9 €

Driving Directions from Paris: Take the A13 motorway, then the A12 to St. Quentin Yvelines Dreux and follow the signs to Elancourt France Miniature.

Public Transportation: Take the La Verrière train from la Défense or Paris Montparnasse station to Elancourt, then take the 411 bus, which stops at France Miniature. You will be able to buy a ticket that includes transportation and the entrance fee at the train stations. This costs 18 € for adults, 15.40 € for children ten to sixteen, and 10.75 for children four to nine.

A miniature replica of France and over 200 of its monuments, including cathedrals, abbeys, and small villages. These are all reduced to a thirtieth of their size, so they are a perfect height for kids. It is open from March 15 to November 16 and is near the Palace of Versailles. My kids especially liked the small, perfect boats, cars, trains, and fairs. If you rent a car for the day, you can combine it with *Thoiry*. It's all outdoors – so go in good weather!

Catacombs
1 place Denfert-Rochereau
75014 Paris
Tel: 01-43-22-47-63
Métro: Denfert-Rocherereau
Adults: 5 €
Hours: Tuesday through Friday, 2 to 4 p.m.
Saturday and Sunday, 9 to 11 a.m. and 2 to 4 p.m.

My kids would totally freak. I wouldn't take children here. It's basically an underground cemetery full of skeletons. The catacombs were quarries during the Middle Ages, but became a graveyard in 1785 when overcrowded cemeteries were considered a health hazard. During World War II, this was the headquarters of the French Resistance.

Boat Trips

Bateaux-Mouches
Pont D'Alma
75008 Paris
Tel: 01-40-76-99-99
Métro: Alma Marceau
Adults: 7 €
Children under twelve: 4 €

These huge boats leave every half hour during the day. The cruises are generally a little over an hour, and are a fantastic way to get an overview of the city and many of its monuments. There is commentary in six languages, including English. There are also lunch (12:15) and dinner (7:45) cruises, which are more expensive and must be reserved.

Les Bateaux Parisiens
Port La Bouronnais
75007 Paris
Tel: 01-44-11-33-44
Boarding points:
Eiffel Tower: porte de la Bouronnais, Métro Trocadéro or Alma Marceau
Notre Dame: quai de Montebello, Métro Saint-Michel or Maubert-Mutualite
Adults: 9.50 €
Children under twelve: 5 €

This company offers two tours – one an Eiffel Tower trip and the other a Notre Dame cruise. These are both about an hour and have audio in English as well as many other languages. There are also dinner and lunch cruises, which are more expensive and require reservations. Don't attempt to take the boat to see the Bastille Day fireworks. It's a madhouse.

Les Vedettes du Pont Neuf
Square du Vert-Galant
75001 Paris
Tel: 01-46-33-98-38
Métro: Pont Neuf or Louvre
Adults: 10 €
Children four to twelve: 5 €

Another one-hour Seine cruise that goes past all the sites. From March to October they leave every half-hour, and every forty-five minutes the rest of the year. There is a lunch cruise for 45 € and two classes of dinner cruise for 49 € and 64 €. You must reserve for these cruises.

Bat-o-bus

This is basically a boat-bus service that runs down the Seine. It has eight stops: Louvre, Jardin des Plantes, Nôtre Dame, Hotel De Ville, Champs Elysées, Musée D'Orsay, St. Germain des Pres and Tour Eiffel. You can buy a one-day ticket for 11 € (children are 5 €).

Fun Fairs

They aren't kidding. These are really fun. If you're in Paris for one of these, be sure to take your children, especially if you are skipping Disneyland. The opening and closing dates may vary, so check with the tourist office or your hotel.

La Fête des Tuileries
A fair in the Tuileries park from mid-June through late August.
Métro: Concorde, Tuileries

La Faire du Trône
This carnival is in the Pelouse de Reuilly section of the Bois de Vincennes from the end of April through May.
Métro: Porte Dorée, Charenton-Liberte

La Fete a Neu-Neu
A fun fair near the Bois de Boulogne, which lasts from early September through the beginning of October.
Métro: Porte de la Muette

Toy Stores

Au Bon Marché
5 rue Babylone
75007 Paris
Métro: Sèvres-Babylone
Tel: 01-44-39-80-00
Hours: Monday through Saturday from 9:30 a.m. to 7 p.m.

This department store has a large toy section in its basement with just about everything.

Au Nain Bleu
408 rue Saint-Honoré
75008 Paris
Tel: 01-42-60-39-01
Métro: Madeline
Hours: Monday through Saturday from 9:45 a.m. to 6:30 p.m.

A fancy, expensive toy store comparable to FAO Schwarz.

Baby Rêve
32 av. Rapp
75007 Paris
Tel: 01-45-51-24-00
Métro: Ecole Militaire
Hours: Tuesday through Saturday from 10 a.m. to 7 p.m.

This store carries a lot of educational toys and terrific baby dolls.

La Grande Recré
Centre cial Italie
2-30 av. d'Italie
75013 Paris
Tel: 01-53-62-15-12
Métro: Place d'Italie
Hours: Mondays through Saturday from 10 a.m. to 7:30 p.m.

Major Barbie, Lego, and video game inventory.

Le Ciel est à Toute la Monde
Kaleidoscopes, Frisbees, boomerangs, toys unique to France and complete collection of Little Prince stationery.

Locations:
Carrousel du Louvre
99 rue de Rivoli
75001 Paris
Métro: Palais-Royale-Musée du Louvre
Tel: 01-49-27-93-03
Hours: Every day but Tuesday from 10 a.m. to 8 p.m.

L'Epée des Bois
12 rue 'Epée-des-Bois
75005 Paris
Tel: 01-43-31-50-18
Métro: Monge or Censier Daubenton

Le Joie Pour Tous
37 bd. Saint-Germain
75005 Paris
Tel: 01-43-54-98-67
Métro: Maubert Mutualité
Hours: 10 a.m. to 7 p.m.

A well-stocked supply of radio-controlled boats, yo-yos, action figures, Fisher Price roller-skates, cars, costumes, masks, soccer balls, bubbles, squirt guns, balloons, and more. Check on lunch closing.

Le Monde en Marche
34 rue Dauphine
75006 Paris
Tel: 01-43-29-09-49
Métro: Odéon
Hours: Monday through Saturdays from 10:30 a.m. to 7:30 p.m.

Music boxes, kites, nature kits, wooden toys, and more.

Il Était une Fois
1 rue Cassette
75006 Paris
Tel: 01-45-48-21-10
Métro: St-Sulpice
Hours: Open Monday, 12 noon to 7:30 p.m.
Tuesday through Saturday open from 10 a.m. to 7:30 p.m.

This homey store carries small playthings and a lot of wooden toys. It also has the Little Prince line – the watches, T-shirts, plates, and cups. The t-shirts and watches are wonderful. You'll also find Babar and TinTin clothes here, as well as assorted backpacks.

Clothing Stores

I could take up an entire book with kids' clothing stores, so I'm just mentioning my favorites and the traditional mainstays. French sizes are different. Size one is really for an average one-year-old, etc.

Du Pareil au Même Kids

Cheap chic for kids – and my favorite for children's clothing. You'll see it all over Paris. It's worth waiting for if your kids need some clothes. They have great t-shirts and wonderful baby clothes. The prices are less than the Gap, and you can bring home a French dress. One of my boys is addicted to Du Pareil au Même pajamas.

A few of its locations:

168 bd. Saint-Germain
75006 Paris

14 rue St. Placide
75006 Paris

15/17 rue des Mathurins
75008 Paris

97 av. Victor-Hugo
75016 Paris

Cyrillus

Preppy and more expensive, this is the place for adorable smocked dresses or a special jacket. It has boys', girls', men's, and women's clothes. The store also has a catalogue it will send to the United States. A few locations:

16 rue de Sèvres (there is a Lego table here where children can play while you shop)
75006 Paris

11-13 av. Duquesne
75007 Paris

8 rue Chanez
750116 Paris

Chattawak

Good coordinated basics. In the winter, pull-on cords and little sweatshirts. Sizes two to twelve.
A few locations:
125 rue Saint Dominique
75007 Paris

30 rue des Saints-Pères
75007 Paris

8 rue Guichard
75016 Paris

Tartine et Chocolate

This store has adorable clothing for sizes up to twelve. It also carries baby furniture, accessories, dolls, baby perfume, and candy (for baptisms).
Locations:

266 bd. Saint-Germain
75007 Paris

24 rue de la Paix
75002 Paris

105 rue Faubourg Saint-Honoré
75008 Paris

60 av. Paul-Doumer
75016 Paris

Bonpoint

The classic French store where society children are outfitted (newborn through eighteen years). Special and very expensive.
A few locations:
320 rue St. Honoré
75001 Paris

50 rue Etienne Marcel
75002 Paris

Jacadi

In the U.S., Jacadi is known for its baby clothes, but here, the stores carry up to children's size sixteen. You'll find preppy classics and adorable smocked dresses.
A few of the locations:
4 av. des Gobelins
75005 Paris

73 rue des Sèvres
75006 Paris

76 rue d'Assas
75006 Paris

256 bd. Saint-Germain
75007 Paris

114 rue de La-Fontaine
750116 Paris

Petit Faune

33 rue Jacob and 89 rue des Rennes
75006 Paris

The kind of place that makes you want to have another one. Wonderful, expensive outfits for babies and small children (up to size eight).

Agnès B

2 rue du Jour
75001 Paris
Métro: Les Halles
Hours: Monday through Saturday, 10 a.m. to 7:30 p.m.

Known for Agnès B adult clothes, this store carries outfits for newborns through fourteen. Agnès B has great cotton outfits and T-shirts and cute hats, socks and other little things.

Sonia Rykial Enfant

4 rue de Grenelle
75006 Paris

Couture for kids. Sonia Rykial designs in miniature (up to twelve). Most of it is casual and comfortable. The store also carries a lot of accessories.

Petit Bateau

Known for soft cottons, and in the U.S. for baby wear, the stores actually carry up to children's size sixteen. I wear Petit Bateau t-shirts, which are cheap and wonderful.

A few locations:
81 rue de Sèvres
75006 Paris

13 rue Tronchet
75008 Paris

64 av. Victor-Hugo
75016 Paris

La Boutique de Floraine

Here, you'll find an adorable collection of Babar and TinTin clothes.
Locations:
176 rue de Grenelle
75007 Paris

87 rue de Longchamp
750116 Paris

Just in Case You Need It: Health

There is nothing worse than having a sick child away from home. The American Hospital has a pediatrics center that is open Monday through Friday from 9 a.m. to 8 p.m., and Saturday from 9 a.m. to 2 p.m. To make an appointment, call: 01-46-41-27-67. The hospital is on the edge of the sixteenth arrondissement in a suburb called Neuilly. Take a taxi there. The pediatrics center is located near the emergency room entrance. There are plenty of cabs lined up outside when you want to go home. Please note that the American Hospital does not provide pediatric emergency services. If you have an emergency, you need to go to one of the emergency rooms at the children's hospitals listed below. The Hôpital Necker Enfants Malades and the Hôpital Saint Vincent de Paul have some arrangements with the American Hospital. To call an ambulance, dial 15.

Hospitals with an English-speaking staff

Hôpital Américan
63 bd. Victor Hugo
92 Neuilly
Tel: 01-46-41-25-25

Hôpital Franco Britannique
3 rue Barbes
92 Levallois Perret
Tel: 01-46-39-22-22

Children's Hospitals

Hôpital Robert-Debre
48 bd. Serurier
75019 Paris
Tel: 01-40-03-20-00

Hôpital Necker Enfants Malades
149 rue de Sévres
75015 Paris
Tel: 01-44-49-40-00

Hôpital d'Enfants Armand Trousseau
26 av. du Dr-Arnold-Netter
75012 Paris
Tel: 01-44-73-74-75

Hôpital Saint-Vincent-de-Paul
82 av. Denfert-Rochereau
75014 Paris
Tel: 01-40-48-81-11

Doctors

SOS help
Tel: 01-46-21-46-46
English-speaking hotline.

SOS Medecins (doctors)
House calls
Tel: 01-47-07-77-77

SOS Cardiology
Tel: 01-47-07-50-50

SOS Dentiste
Tel: 01-43-37-51-00

If you have a dental emergency at night, weekend, or holiday. The American Hospital also has emergency dental services.

Emergency Numbers:

Ambulance
Tel: 15

Fire
Tel: 18

Poison Control
Tel: 01-40-37-04-04

Police
Tel: 17

Burns
Urgent: 01-44-73-64-07
Nonurgent: 01-44-73-74-75

24-Hour Pharmacies

By law, each arrondissement must have a pharmacy open all night. These rotate, but the information for an open pharmacy will be in all pharmacy windows. This also applies to Sunday. There are also a few pharmacies that are open twenty-four hours or late hours on a full-time basis. These are listed below. Pharmacies have a green cross as a sign.

24 Hours

Pharmacie des Champs
84 av. des Champs-Elysées
75008 Paris
Tel: 01-45-62-02-41
Métro: Georges V

Pharmacie Européenne
Place de Clichy
75009 Paris
Tel: 01-48-74-65-18
Métro: Place de Clichy

Late Hours:

Pharmacie Opéra-Capucines
6 bd. des Capucines
75009 Paris
Tel: 01-42-65-88-29
Métro: Opéra
Open until midnight every night.

Pharmacie des Halles
10 bd. de Sébastopol
75004 Paris
Tel: 01-42-72-03-23
Métro: Chatelet
Open every day until midnight.

Pharmacie des Arts
106 bd. de Montparnasse
75014 Paris
Tel: 01-43-35-44-88
Métro: Montparanasse-Bienvenue
Open until midnight every day.

Pharmacie Matignon
2 rue Jean Mermoz
75008 Paris
Tel: 01-43-59-86-55
Métro: Opéra
Open 365 days a year from 8:30 a.m. until 2 a.m.

English-Speaking Pharmacies

Pharmacie Anglo-Américaine
37 av. Marceau
75016 Paris
Tel: 01-47-20-57-37
Métro: Tuileries
Hours: Monday through Saturday from 9 a.m. to 7:30 p.m.

British and American Pharmacy
1 rue Auber
75009 Paris
Tel: 01-42-65-88-29
Métro: Opéra or Hauve-Caumartin
Hours: Monday through Friday, 8:30 a.m. to 8 p.m. and 10 a.m. to 8 p.m. on Saturday

Printed in the United States
93929LV00002B/79-90/A